POST
BLACK

POST BLACK

HOW A NEW GENERATION IS REDEFINING
AFRICAN AMERICAN IDENTITY

YTASHA L. WOMACK

Foreword by Derek T. Dingle, Editor in Chief, *Black Enterprise*

Lawrence Hill Books

Library of Congress Cataloging-in-Publication Data
Womack, Ytasha.
Post black : how a new generation is redefining African American identity
/ Ytasha L. Womack.
    p. cm.
Includes bibliographical references and index.
ISBN 978-1-55652-805-7 (pbk.)
1. African Americans—Race identity. 2. African Americans—Social condi-
tions—21st century. 3. Identity (Psychology) I. Title.

E185.625.W595 2010
305.896'073—dc22

                                                2009029619

Cover and interior design: Visible Logic, Inc.
Interior illustrations: *Biracial Identity*, *Spiritual Evolution*, and *Neofeminism*
© Craig J. Stevenson; *Generation Gap* and *Talented Tenth* © John Jennings;
African Diaspora and *Entrepreneur Revolution* © Cory J. Stevenson; *K-OSS* ©
Digital Noixe Production; *Duke of Rap* © Nathaniel Quinn

Published by Lawrence Hill Books
An imprint of Chicago Review Press, Incorporated
814 North Franklin Street
Chicago, Illinois 60610
ISBN 978-1-55652-805-7
Printed in the United States of America
5 4 3 2 1

This book is dedicated to those with vision, passion, and perseverance who believe in goodwill and have the courage to follow their path—to those who don't let others define them, but create a life all their own.

It is very exciting and interesting to read about famous and creative people. But it is merely entertainment if we simply read and do not identify with those qualities that created this success.

—Tom Johnson, minister, author, lecturer

CONTENTS

FOREWORD
A NEW AGE

Something is profoundly different about America today from the nation we had all been living in prior to November 4, 2008, when Americans elected Barack Obama president of the United States. Unlike members of the civil rights generation, I was not of the camp that believed I would never witness an American of African heritage in the Oval Office in my lifetime. I felt it was possible. But that still did not stop me from becoming overwhelmed with emotion on election night.

It was an important event for African Americans, certainly. But watching the throngs of supporters celebrating in Chicago's Grant Park as well as the stunning response from people across the nation and around the world, I saw clearly that Obama's victory belonged to a tapestry of humanity. It belonged to every American who refused to accept the idea that cultural and racial differences are insurmountable. It belonged to every American with the courage to leap beyond stereotypes and outmoded ideas about race. It belonged to everyone who rejects the slash-and-burn politics of negativity and embraces the idea that collectively we can be better.

I like to think that it was the courage, ambition, and sacrifice of African American achievers throughout our history—from law to medicine to the arts—and supporters of civil rights that in 2008 allowed Americans of all races and backgrounds to set aside their divisions and embrace Obama's message of change.

But I also believe that it was young people—a generation of Americans that has come of age unencumbered by the same racial baggage of their elders—that are the real heroes of that moment in history. The political pundits were wrong. The generation that many had written off got serious, got organized, got involved, and delivered the most remarkable and resounding political victory in this nation's history. For them, electing a black president was possible because they were born too late to be poisoned by the idea that it wasn't.

Since the election, President Obama and our beautiful black first family has been the image of America transmitted across the globe. The unprecedented whistle-stop tour, the historic inauguration ceremony, and the celebrated trip to Europe provided the world community with a sight never seen before—a black man of confidence, intellect, and grace not only as part of the global arena but assuming the mantle of Leader of the Free World.

So has the revelry of his ascension to the presidency signaled the long-awaited arrival of a "postracial" America? One has to admit that it's a compelling and attractive concept—the idea that after centuries of political and spiritual conflict, a nation went to the polls and in one glorious, transformative act literally purged the land of the scourges of racism, exclusion, and discord. Yes, it is a romantic notion. Of course, we all know that social change is never that easy. Indeed, if we learned anything from the remarkable unfolding of the Obama presidency, it was that issues of race run deep in our culture, institutions, and national psyche.

During the presidential campaign, when senator John McCain in one of his stump speeches asked his audience "Who is Barack Obama?" he elicited angry jeers and calls for violence that startled many, including the senator himself. That moment and others like it throughout the contest were stark reminders that long-held race-based fears and suspicions are still very much with us. We belittle or ignore them at our peril.

Even more telling, to my mind, at least, was the question it-self: *Who is Barack Obama?* Implicit in Senator McCain's rhetorical query was the idea that his opponent somehow didn't belong in contention for the highest office in the land. Not because he wasn't smart or capable or because he lacked the qualities of leadership but because he was somehow "not one of us"—a message underscored by the concurrent whisper campaign about Obama's possibly being a Muslim with links to terrorists or perhaps not an American citizen at all. And let's not forget vice-presidential candidate Governor Sarah Palin's pointed appeal to so-called real Americans. Certainly the intent of all this was to tap into some voters' suspicions about Obama and his background as if his very presence in the race had broken some unspoken, unwritten rule about who and what a U.S. president should be. It was race-baiting of the worst kind and familiar to anyone with a rudimentary knowledge of the history of race in electoral politics. The stoking of white fear and resentment has been a campaign staple from the postslavery period of Reconstruction to the modern evolution of late Republican president Richard M. Nixon's infamous "Southern strategy" that had tipped the scales in favor of Republican candidates for almost three decades.

Only this time, it failed. Indeed, the strategy failed so spectacularly in 2008 that it's clear that something transformational did, in fact, happen on November 4. America turned a page on the matter of race. The question before us is *Have we at long last closed the book?*

I believe a good place to start in examining this question is that historic election night when Barack Hussein Obama opened an audacious chapter in the history books. If you watched the results on TV or online, then you saw in those ecstatic faces the seeds of that victory—something Governor Palin and others had been blind to—and that victory is that in the early twenty-first century the "real" America is a diverse America.

Obama's achievement had given voice to a new era—one that you will become familiar with on the following pages of this book. Shifting demographics over the past two decades have reshaped our nation's racial and ethnic landscape in profound ways. It's estimated that within a generation the collective population of so-called minorities—African Americans, Latinos, and Asians—will surpass that of white Americans. At *Black Enterprise*, we have been writing about this trend for years in terms of its ramifications for corporate America's practices and priorities. Our magazine was among the earliest and most vocal advocates for diversity initiatives as an economic imperative for industries that want to stay competitive in a powerfully diverse marketplace.

The implications for the political landscape are equally profound and helped make Obama—with his biracial heritage, international upbringing, broad education, and history of public service—the ideal candidate for his time. The details of his victory confirm this. In the popular vote, more than 66 million Americans (53 percent of voters) cast their ballots for Obama, who received 95 percent of the black vote, 43 percent of the white vote, and 66 percent of the Hispanic vote—the highest numbers ever for a Democrat. Just as important, he brought a new generation to the polls, capturing 66 percent of voters under thirty and 71 percent of first-time voters. In doing so, he redrew the electoral map, winning so-called red states such as Indiana and North Carolina. And here's the irony for the smear-throwers during the campaign: in today's contemporary context, Barack Obama probably won the election because in a field of mostly white, mostly male, mostly older contenders he was "most" American.

It didn't happen overnight, of course. The broadening acceptance of African Americans in leadership roles has been a focus of *Black Enterprise* since the magazine's inception four decades ago. It can be well argued that the evolution of the African American business and professional class has been the primary catalyst for this development. In 1987, financier Reginald F. Lewis made history as the first black entrepreneur to structure a nearly billion-dollar leveraged buyout to create TLC Beatrice International, the first black-owned business to generate more than two billion dollars in gross sales and control divisions in the United Kingdom, France, Ireland, and Australia. Lewis, a Baltimore native and graduate of the HBCU (historically black college and university) Virginia State University and Harvard Law School, viewed himself not solely as an African American but a citizen of the world. Roughly twenty years later, in 2009, *Black Enterprise* published its annual list of the 100 Most Powerful African American Executives, including twenty CEOs who collectively oversee billions in corporate assets and exert enormous power across the globe. So when a Ken Chenault, chairman and CEO of American Express, sits at the helm of a global conglomerate, it redefines the mainstream's idea of what African Americans are capable of achieving. And where business goes, government follows. Say what you will about the policies of president George W. Bush, his appointments of Colin Powell and Condoleezza Rice to power positions helped make an Obama presidency that much more plausible.

The nature of Obama's appeal to white and minority voters is worth noting as another example of how the nation has turned a corner on race. Candidate Obama did not run from his race to appeal to a broad coalition of voters, but neither did he permit race to define him or his message. He was not a "race card" candidate who spoke the language of victimhood, white guilt, or what was owed for past injustice. To black audiences, his was a challenging voice, not a coddling one. To white audiences, he offered calm reassurance that he understood the issues that were important to them.

Crucially, he spoke directly to the middle class and focused on issues that transcend race—health care, the economy, and the human
cost of an unpopular war. When he did address race, as he did in
response to the flap over the inflammatory comments of his former
pastor Jeremiah Wright, he did so with a maturity and openness of
vision that was unprecedented for a public official of any race.

His compelling dissertation on race in America will be remembered, dissected, and quoted for decades. It has already earned a
place in what will be his presidential legacy because of the deft way
it contextualized both the anger expressed by African Americans
of Reverend Wright's generation and that of working-class white
Americans who feel unfairly burdened with the responsibility for
past sins. This excerpt is especially noteworthy:

> *Just as black anger often proved counterproductive*
> *so have these white resentments distracted attention*
> *from the real culprits of the middle-class squeeze—a*
> *corporate culture rife with inside dealing, question-*
> *able accounting practices, and short-term greed; a*
> *Washington dominated by lobbyists and special*
> *interests; economic policies that favor the few over*
> *the many. And yet, to wish away the resentments*
> *of white Americans, to label them as misguided or*
> *even racist, without recognizing they are grounded*
> *in legitimate concerns—this too widens the racial*
> *divide and blocks the path to understanding.*

Here was a black elected official boldly attempting to broach understanding with a demographic that conventional wisdom dictated
was least likely to vote for him and identifying common ground—a
basis for forging unity based on common interest. It was a perfor-
mance that left many voters across the racial spectrum feeling empowered and confident that here was a candidate of presidential timbre.

That's not to say that institutional racism is not still alive and operating in America. Even in the age of Obama, African Americans and Hispanic Americans are still more likely than white Americans to be poor and unemployed, be denied quality health care, and receive a substandard education. A recent Pew study revealed that one in nine African American males age twenty to thirty-four is incarcerated. And with the ashen state of the economy pushing so many families, businesses, and institutions to the brink of disaster, it's easy to imagine that the social progress many of us take for granted could recede. Politically, economically, and socially, more and more Americans could be shut out of the promise of opportunity and pushed back into society's margins. If that happens, the racial divisions that were seemingly overcome with Obama's multicultural, multiracial, multigenerational Election Day mandate may reappear.

But those facts don't erase the promise of November 4, 2008. In his victory speech in Chicago's Grant Park, Obama proclaimed: "It's been a long time coming but tonight, because of what we did on this day, in this election, at this defining moment, change has come to America." Since that shining moment, his ethos of cultural inclusion and policies of financial and ethical restoration has ushered in a new era. He has also effectively shattered the myth of the black monolith—the misguided notion that blacks have only been spawned from one experience. You only have to look at his life, his family, and his inner circle to bear witness to that fallacy: he's the product of a Kenyan father and a white Kansas-bred mother and was reared in Hawaii; first lady Michelle, who can trace her roots to pre–Civil War South Carolina where her paternal great-great-grandfather was a slave, was raised on Chicago's South Side by two black parents; and one of his chief advisers and closest friends, Valerie Jarrett, whose father was a pathologist-geneticist, was born in Iran and spoke Persian and French as a child.

Although America may not be a postracial society, could it be post black? In a nation that witnessed the desegregation of public schools through the Supreme Court decision in *Brown v. Board of Education* fifty-five years ago, the assassination of Dr. Martin Luther King Jr. more than forty years ago, the Los Angeles riots seventeen years ago, and one of the world's great cities almost drowned because of cataclysmic government indifference to its largely black and brown inhabitants almost a half decade ago, the nation has taken some evolutionary steps. And with them, it has started discarding its limited view of the definition and capabilities of blacks in our society and our world.

So what now? I, for one, am looking ahead with renewed optimism. I believe that the age of Obama has effectively spawned the twenty-first century. He has brought a new generation to power, brought an end to baby boomer domination of politics, business, and social affairs. Now a phalanx of energetic, change-oriented postboomers, Gen Xers, Gen Yers, and millennials will take charge of the decades ahead. It may be a generation or so after the end of his term before history can truly evaluate the full extent of the Obama effect. One thing is certain, however. This really is a new epoch to be someone of color in America in terms of economic and social advancement, impact on the larger culture, and identity—our sense of who we are and how we view ourselves. These times demand remarkable individuals, men and women of courage and perception who see the world as their playing field. Those who are prepared to ride the cusp of rapid change and identify what the twenty-first century requires and deliver. You'll find such examples on the pages of *Post Black*.

Derek Dingle

Editor of *Black Enterprise*

INTRODUCTION
IDENTITY THEFT

This is not a book about despair in black America.

In this book, I will not detail every pathological condition that ever existed in African American life. You won't read about the "endangered black male," "the destruction of the black family," or "the welfare queen." It is not a diatribe on the proliferation of drug kingpins, crack addicts, gang violence, or unemployment in the inner cities. Nor is it a bashing of the single mother, a study of the absent father, or a condemnation of troubled youth.

Not that I'm making light of these issues. These are grave matters. But there are people dedicated to keeping these poignant topics on the kitchen table of America's hearts and at the forefront of its remote-control consciousness. They have studied and restudied these issues, shaken them up in the test tube of life, and flapjacked them under the microscope of public scrutiny. They have stomach-pumped the data to the point of resuscitation, forcing people to do something about these issues, which is why you will surely hear these discussions whether I choose to write about them or not.

They are realities, make no mistake about it. But they are not the only realities in black life.

And if you thought I was blindsided by optimism, using my college education as a gateway to escapism, or turning an elitist eye toward the globe's challenges, you're wrong. I know that we're all interconnected.

I am fully aware that I live in the city of Chicago, home to the second-largest African American community in the country, birthplace of the black-born staples the blues, gospel, *Ebony*, and *Jet*. The home of house music. The city that bred Harold Washington and the nation's only two black senators since Reconstruction. The place where two black men launched bids for president. The place where both Jesse Jackson Sr. and Louis Farrakhan live in peace. The place where Fred Hampton was killed in cold blood. The old El Rukins territory. Home to the Bud Billiken Parade. Land of mild sauce. The city Oprah calls home.

And if I didn't know I lived here, I've got a closet full of oversized winter coats, a pair of fur boots (sorry, PETA), and a stack of metered parking tickets to prove it.

If by some strike of cultural amnesia you missed the memo, or the latest updates on these issues on the edited evening news, no worries, because people are talking about them. Everyone is talking about them. Black people are talking about them. I'll go so far as to say you can't get away from it even if you tried . . . the conversation, that is. We talk about these issues in our living rooms; in college dorms; at picnics; in barbershops, beauty shops, churches, and chat rooms; in soul food diners and cafés; on stoops and porches; in bars and bowling alleys. We talk about these issues at work. Some of us talk about these issues in our sleep.

We debate them; we argue them. We get fired up. Sometimes we laugh to keep from crying. Sometimes we live them.

But I digress.

This book is not about the dearth of "good black men." It's not a literary lynching of "the gold digger." It's not a broadside criticism of pretty women in videos. Or platinum grills on men. This book is not about rims. This book is not an ode to "the good old days." It is not a waxing nostalgic about the days before desegregation, the mythical days when "real community values" ruled and everyone lived holier-than-thou lives and marched to the beat of freedom. Nor is this a sentimental dedication to the thrills of thug life. It's not about flashy pimps or smooth-talking hustlers, ladies with telltale hearts, or men with eyes that kill.

This book is not a call for black love.

Nor is it a call for black leadership.

And I'm not asking you to be a role model.

This book is not about rap icons or sports figures.

THIS BOOK IS NOT ABOUT RAP ICONS OR SPORTS FIGURES.

This book will not blame hip-hop for society's ills.

It won't nitpick at civil rights failures (I'm not an ingrate).

Nor will this book uphold heroes you already know about. Heroes you should know about.

I will not use black people as the poster children for America's issues.

I will not conclude that prayer is the answer. And yes, I go to church.

And I won't recommend that Bill Cosby, Oprah, and Michael Jordan get together and solve the world's problems. I won't explore conspiracy theories. Some have merit; I just won't discuss them.

I won't define the word "ghetto." I won't define "life in the 'hood." And just in case you're confused, this book is not black erotica. This book is not street lit. I won't question what happened to that money collected at the Million Man March. And I won't mention O.J.

So what, you ask, is a book about African Americans about if it's not discussing any of the above?

I'll get back to that.

REWIND: DAWN OF THE NEW MILLENNIUM

I was a fresh-faced reporter heralding from Clark Atlanta University, and my neo–Black Power training in the age of music videos and It bags made me a fashionable Ida B. Wells zealot with the naïveté of Lois Lane. I had decided during my senior year of high school that I would write about areas of black life that weren't showcased in the mainstream media, that other half of the story that all too often got lost in the midst of subtle racism and the rat race shuffle. The winds of change that ushered in the new millennium made for the perfect writer's training ground, 'cause a change was coming. Dollar signs punctuated the clouds hovering over the heads of the black aspirational ranks who knew that the right idea at the right time could make them wealthy. Ideas doubled as currency for those with short money, and a cadre of African Americans was adamant that it was a shout-out away from being a filthy rich juggernaut whose work would forever change the lot of blacks in America. If the late Reginald Lewis, famed for the Beatrice Foods takeover, could do it, so could we. If P. Diddy, then Puff Daddy, could become a household name, so could we. Or at least that's the way it seemed.

Civil rights organizations charged that the final frontier of the movement would be economic. The Rainbow PUSH Coalition launched the Wall Street Project, a three-day conference complete with parties at the New York Stock Exchange attended by celebrities, investment bankers, CEOs, and small business owners all hobnobbing with their eyes on the economic prize. Housing projects, a well-worn symbol of America's unkept promise, were bulldozed to the cheers and fears of neighbors who questioned the changes to come. Forgotten zones in black areas rife with warehouses and poverty emerged, hot properties for hungry real estate agents. Homeowners talked of owning strip malls. People who'd never so much as read the *Wall Street Journal* learned to invest in stocks. And it seemed like everyone wanted to start their own business in hopes of "revitalizing the community."

And there were other inklings of change to note. Diversity management replaced affirmative action debates. "Urban" morphed from a coded marketing term for "black" and became a symbol for hipsters influenced by black lifestyles; hip-hop, the voice of the streets, got a platinum and chinchilla makeover, becoming forever etched in mainstream status; and the grassroots marketing techniques that used to launch political candidates and underground music became corporate America's most effective means to reach young consumers. Despite a dot-com bust that saw inflated virtual treasures plummet, the Internet emerged unscathed and quickly established itself as the premiere tool to revolutionize business. Mobile offices became standard, and a steady laptop and cell phone could patch you in to a multimillion-dollar deal on the other side of the world.

The arts world also launched a new-school revolution of sorts. Aspiring musicians wanted to start their own labels. People who'd never set foot in the Ivy League halls of MBA-land felt perfectly confident that they could found multimillion-dollar enterprises. The churchgoing audience that had long been ignored by the mainstream was supporting new gospel plays en masse, making millionaires and legends out of neighborhood playwrights. A poetry revival stoked the flames of passion, and modern wordsmiths became local superstars.

I worked at the *Chicago Defender*. The nation's oldest and only (at the time) black-owned daily paper, the *Defender* had soared to prominence with the emergence of another black culture shift: the Great Migration. This radical flocking of Southern-born blacks to the North between 1920 and the 1970s ushered in the paper's golden age. The *Chicago Defender* filled its coffers by documenting the thriving businesses and society life of these "new Negroes" and was the leading African American newspaper advocating for equal rights. But at the dawn of the new millennium, the paper had become a shadow of its former self. Critics charged that it had lost touch, a critique that saddened the die-hard staff but reflected its struggles to make sense of new technology and new ideas spawned by people who weren't linked to old-guard affiliations. The paper's longstanding emphasis on local politics, public housing, and do-good citizens and social clubs was once a revolutionary stance. But now these topics represented just a small slice of the worldly issues capturing the hearts and imaginations of Chicago's African American readers, who could just as easily read stories on black life online and in mainstream papers.

The *Defender* office was a unique space. The all-black reporting staff was a model of lifestyle diversity. It included a rotating cast of rogue individualists—a self-proclaimed libertarian editor, a symphony-loving music writer, two punk rockers, a heavy metal head, recent HBCU grads, an antagonistic Vietnam War vet, a Gulf War veteran who hated HBCUs, two Republicans, an agnostic, a Black Israelite, a former prostitute, a convicted felon, an African immigrant, a Puerto Rican college student, and an administrative assistant who'd just gotten off welfare. And during a time when hip-hop's millions eclipsed country music in sales, 90 percent of the staff thought hip-hop was as creative as a ham sandwich, with the Vietnam War vet, metal heads, and concerto lover quadruple-teaming me whenever the subject surfaced. They were a lovable bunch who worked for pennies but were fueled by writing about African American life. We were headed by Colonel Eugene Scott, another war veteran who led this argumentative band of troops from one battle-rich issue to the next.

I was given a wide range of freedoms and allowed to develop stories as I wished: "Black Businesses on the Rise," "Southside Native Founds Hip-Hop Magazine," "Black Spending Power at All-Time High," "Black Investors Growing." I wrote about new health issues in the community, new trends in entertainment, business issues, and African American markets. But these stories stood in stark contrast to the rest of the news features—a rotating saga of city politics, crime, and familiar social issues. While my boss and colleagues were pleased with my diligence, they found my stories, while intriguing, to be niche features at best. In the minds of many, I was writing enthusiastically about topics that most black people, aka the *real* black people, simply weren't into.

I wish I could say I was surprised. But despite the diversity of this motley crew, which waged all-out standoffs on everything from voting rights to existentialism, few could see how their own differences reflected a growing diversity among African Americans at large. Or maybe they did see it, but the leadership at the time didn't know how or if these viewpoints should be integrated into their homogenous coverage of black life.

Readers demanded more, because African American life encompassed so much more. Times were changing, yet there was a death-grip hold on a cookie-cutter image of black life that just didn't apply to every person of African descent living in America. Studies, living witnesses, and testimonies proving otherwise couldn't wedge a dent in this tried-and-true image, and I didn't understand why.

I had to convince our argumentative sports editor that my high school, Whitney M. Young, a top-ranking magnet school of national acclaim, was mostly black. He didn't believe me. Eventually he caved in, giving some credence to the fact that I once attended the institution. "But it's not a *real* black school," he chimed. He was joking, but he wasn't joking. What is a real black school? I wondered. And why is it that any shining example of achievement among African Americans is viewed as some abnormality rather than a trend or a building block? Why aren't "scholastic excellence" and "African American" considered synonymous, despite living examples?

These sentiments were echoed when I wrote a piece on support centers that complemented medical treatment for HIV. HIV rates were rising in African American communities, and I dedicated a lot of stories to the issue. With alternative health practices going mainstream, this well-meaning center attracted a growing number of African American clients and wanted to educate blacks on their free services, which included massages, yoga, meditation classes, and Reiki. The editor at the time took one look at the story and I could feel the steam rising from his temples. The story could stay, but Reiki, a Tibetan Buddhist healing art, had to go. "Black people don't know what Reiki is," he said. Most people don't know what Reiki is, I said. I didn't know what it was either until I asked the people at the center about it. I couldn't understand what angered him. African Americans with HIV enjoying a free yoga class shouldn't ruffle anyone's feathers. He ran the story, but he wasn't pleased about it. "Black people aren't into this stuff," he scoffed. Yet herbalist stores, yoga workshops, and GNCs were popping up all over the 'hood.

Either way, this team of writers, each a self-proclaimed expert on black life, each proficient in civil rights, was mildly bewildered by my story choices. Stories stating that there are "more black entrepreneurs than ever" didn't make sense to them when so many storefronts on the city's South and West sides were Arab and Korean owned. After a barrage of these cutting-edge stories I was called to task. "Where are they?" asked Colonel Scott. Scott supported my journalistic pursuits and even had me meet with other military personnel to curb my then belief that the military was only a brethren of trained killers. But even he was overwhelmingly puzzled by this mysterious world I kept writing about. "If there are 'so many' black businesses out here, how come I don't see them?" he asked. I explained Internet-based businesses, the home or virtual office, the shift from retail to services, companies that moved from the 'hood to downtown offices—all things I had researched and written about. While my explanations were lofty, they couldn't shake his image of the corner stores and brick-and-mortar businesses that black communities had been built around.

Despite the looming ownership battle that threatened the paper's survival, the *Defender*'s other great challenge was understanding the lifestyles, likes, and dislikes of this amorphous group, people beyond the reach of old-guard affiliations who demanded more from their media. But in the midst of legal woes, no one got around to tapping this audience, and the paper was eventually sold.

I could have chalked up those attitudes to the experiences of that particular staff. But I kept bumping into other unlikely attitudes about black life by black people who had very specific views about what African Americans did and did not do. They would argue you to the death about these views, which often weren't substantiated by anything other than casual observations among friends. While the assumptions that non–African Americans made about the lack of diversity in the black populace were utterly ridiculous, they were at least understandable. To see the same notions among other African Americans, though, appalled me. Consider the twenty-three-year-old med student who claims that all African Americans are Baptist, the forty-year-old black woman who calls biracial Americans "mulatto," the thirty-two-year-old executive who can't wait for property taxes to force out the black working poor, the forty-one-year-old minister who didn't know that black people ski, the twenty-eight-year-old manager who is afraid to mentor teenagers, the forty-year-old banker who says the reported numbers of black gay and bisexual men are "grossly exaggerated." Or the elderly woman who, after reading the party listings in my social column, said she was just happy that young black people had places to go. "What did you think we were doing?" I asked. "I didn't know," she replied. "The only ones I see are the ones drinking in the park."

People not knowing about something is one thing. If a traveler told me there was a town in China made up of a million African American expats and their descendants, I would say, Wow, I didn't know that. If the traveler went on to describe the town, the people, and their history, I, not knowing anything about the place, could only listen and ask questions. If the traveler gave me articles and research proving this town existed, I would be a fool not to acknowledge that what the traveler saw was in fact real and not some fancy fantasy he conjured up to make some point about African Americans on the world stage. But if I went on a rampage, refusing to believe such a town was possible because I hadn't seen it or couldn't figure out how it could come into being, that's a different story. And if I took my bags, went to China, saw the African American people working in this town, and said "Impossible!" and came back home convincing other African Americans that it didn't exist, you would very well question my sanity or my agenda. Then, if these African Americans from China came back to the United States, flooding towns and cities with their combination of Chinese and African American traditions, I could try to ignore it. I could charge that they aren't "real African Americans." I could argue they need to change their ways. I could refuse to speak to them, frightened by their numbers, fearing they'd take my job. But the truth of the matter is they would exist. They would be woven into the fabric of American life, going to schools, renting, buying, working every day, and opening up Chinese soul food restaurants. So if I were to devise a marketing plan for how to reach African American consumers or get more African Americans to join my professional group, mosque, church, school, and so on, I'd miss out on major dollars and insights if I ignored this huge contingency of African Americans from China.

Now this is a fictitious example (unless there really is a group of African American expats living in a small town in China. If you know of such a town, please let me know). But its implications are real.

DON'T CALL IT A COMEBACK

The new diversity in African American life doesn't neatly fit into America's image box. It doesn't neatly fit into black America's box either. If I swore that African immigrants were the nation's highest-educated newcomers, that a black man was building a multibillion-dollar hotel in Vegas, or that young black professionals even existed, there are people—smart people—who would look at me with blank stares. If I told them they could launch a protest via Twitter, they'd faint.

I know because I've told them. And they don't believe me.

Others get plain hellfire mad. As if to speak about "the others" detracts from the hardships of the past and from the challenges facing many today and makes those lives irrelevant. I participated on a panel once about images of black women. I'm sure those in attendance expected the panelists to talk about the usual subjects: throngs of video girls, the depressing state of single parenthood, and the dire opportunities for black women at large. Flipping the script, most of the panelists spoke freely of women entrepreneurs or driven ladies who overcame challenges to achieve success. The audience was largely pleased. Then one man, angry and annoyed, shouted, "Well what about the poor black mother on welfare? What about the black woman with five kids and no education?" She can be successful, too, I added. The man was speechless.

This diversity is unsettling.

Why? Because it just doesn't match up with any of the images on the news, any of the surface activity in the 'hood, any of the fire-and-brimstone speeches, beliefs, or anecdotes that are rampant in black communities. It doesn't make any sense.

REWIND: BACK TO 2007

It's a post-9/11 world. The year that Britney Spears's commando sightings trumped immigration reform, bottled water became an agent of terror on domestic planes, and a good underwire bra could prevent you from making it through federal security gates. And don't wear your pants too low, my hip-hop aficionados—in some U.S. towns you could be forced to do some time in the slammer. Such sag-averse lawmakers apparently believe the fashion trend is a stone's throw away from anarchy.

So, in 2007, who is the African American with the most clout?

Is it the activist son or daughter of a civil rights icon? Is it the worldly business tycoon who leveraged her parents' storefronts into fortune and fame? Is it the rights-fighting beacon of hope, charging for the empowerment of all?

Guess again. Her name is Condoleezza Rice.

Condoleezza Rice, the highest-ranking black person in the U.S. government and arguably the world, an Alabama-born, conservative Republican and George W. Bush's right hand in negotiating the controversial policies in war-torn Iraq, a war that 85 percent of African Americans are against.

But no one's celebrating. Most African Americans are so uncomfortable with her questionable leadership, dour views on human rights, and inattention to black concerns that her accomplishment provokes an embarrassment second only to that felt over Clarence Thomas. *Washington Post* columnist Eugene Robinson put it plainly: "How did she come to a world view so radically different from that of most black Americans? Is she blind, is she in denial, is she confused or what?"

Pessimism is high. A survey by the Pew Research Center says that just one in five blacks, or 20 percent, believe they are better off, the smallest percentage since 1983. Another 29 percent say things have gotten worse, and fewer than half say they expect their prospects to brighten in the future, down from 57 percent in 1986, that hallmark year when Reaganomics' demonizing of affirmative action struck more fear in the hearts of men than Qaddafi.

Optimism rests on senator Barack Obama, a Hawaiian-born son of a Kenyan father and white Kansan mother, the second African American senator since Reconstruction and a leading contender to represent the Democratic Party for president. His raising millions in campaign dollars prompts his black critics, a hodgepodge of long-time Democratic power mongers, to charge that his biracial identity and overwhelming support from elite funders and a nontraditional coalition of donors compromises his allegiance to the black community. *Is he black enough?* becomes the looming question from a sea of possible haters and longtime Hillary Clinton supporters who mount a passive-aggressive challenge to his mercurial rise.

One congregation of bitter black political strategists disputes his popularity and tells an audience of writers, "He'll never win." Furthermore, they add, white voters favor him because "he has a little bit of white in him." This latter charge is a clear throwback to colorism politics and "what decade is this?" dialogues. But it also raises issues about biracial heritage, black authenticity, and the "real African American" experience. But are the naysayers truly concerned about Obama's ability to represent African American interests, or are they just angry that an African American man with no political lineage and a nontraditional upbringing has become a Kennedyesque superstar?

This question of who's black and who isn't morphs again in the wake of immigration protests. Anti-immigration feelings grow to fanatical levels across the country and split people of color as well. Some African Americans who call in to Chicago's WVON radio station in protest of the undocumented workers of Mexican descent don't realize their anti-immigration stance affects other black people, too, including African, Caribbean, and black Latino immigrants. When this issue is brought up, no caller addresses it. Nor do they see the parallels that the radio host, Santita Jackson, daughter of civil rights icon Jesse Jackson, made between the Great Migration and the desires of immigrants coming to the United States for better opportunities. Instead, callers fear that new immigrants will "take their jobs."

But the number of African immigrants has tripled in the past decade, with one *New York Times* article claiming there are more voluntary African immigrants in the United States now than all the Africans brought in during the slave trade. African immigrants are more likely to be educated than any other immigrant group, but integrating into longstanding black communities and politics is a daunting task. The *New York Times* reports that when one Ethiopian-born activist urged a group of black health care professionals and educators who were developing prevention campaigns to incorporate African immigrants into their scope, he was told their campaigns focused strictly on African Americans. "Am I not African American?" he asked. No, they responded.

Mauricio Velasquez, CEO of Diversity Training Group, a Virginia-based diversity strategy group, said he's never seen anything like it. "There are U.S. domestic blacks saying we're more black than Haitians and Dominicans," said Velasquez. Meanwhile, some Caribbean natives in America embrace terms like "Jamaican American" to separate them from their domestic-born brethren. There are also white Americans born in Africa who claim they are more African than African Americans whose ties to the continent ended two hundred years ago. They argue they should be called African Americans, too.

A Liberian-born computer specialist told me he was shocked to learn that all African Americans aren't "all black." This said just weeks after activist Al Sharpton learned that his family was owned by and may be related to ancestors of racist former senator Strom Thurmond, and a genealogist claimed that Barack Obama is a tenth cousin to conservative vice president Dick Cheney. But African American descendants of slaves in the Cherokee Nation can rest assured that they aren't Cherokee, stated the tribe's leaders, who kicked them off the rosters and withdrew benefits.

In September 2007, hundreds of protesters descend upon a tiny town called Jena, Louisiana, to contest the arrest of six African American teens charged with attempted murder after a string of race-baiting incidents, including a noose hanging, leads to what amounts to an after-school fight. Although black youth are frequently charged with not caring about politics, many, in a move reminiscent of the civil rights era, support the nationwide campaign. The protest is waged in an underground fashion not by long-standing civil rights organizations—not at first anyway—but by a coalition of little-known human rights groups and black college students who leveraged what may be the first major civil rights protest launched through the Internet. The yearlong campaign utilizes peer sites including YouTube, MySpace, and Facebook, the same sites maligned by parents of teens, schools, and critics for propagating sexual content. The incident funnels through black media outlets and eventually makes national headlines. But it sparks a reemergence of noose sightings in offices and college campuses across the nation, highlighting a public backlash to progress made by African Americans in the past fifty years. The protest stands apart from others as the first major new millennium protest involving grassroots organizations, black college students, and new media while capturing mainstream attention.

Meanwhile, Stanley O'Neal, one of a handful of African American CEOs helming Fortune 500 companies, after a tumultuous 2007 quarter leaves his position with Merrill Lynch, taking a whopping $161 million worth of stock options and retirement benefits. It's a first for a black CEO, the fifth-highest exit package in history. A week later, Dick Parsons, head of Time Warner, the world's reigning media empire, steps down as well. While these businessmen and their exploits are covered in the likes of *Forbes* and the *Wall Street Journal*, most black people don't know who they are.

They also don't know that R. Don Peebles, a Washington, D.C., native whose multibillion-dollar real estate empire includes the Royal Palm in Miami Beach, prepares to break ground for a two-billion-dollar luxury hotel in Las Vegas. His book, *The Peebles Principles*, guides people of color who seek fortune in the real estate game. He was not born with a silver spoon, he writes, emphasizing that he came from a middle-class, single-parent home. "By the time I was twenty-seven, I was a multimillionaire, and by the time I was forty-five, I was worth more than a quarter of a billion dollars." Oddly, Peebles's success hovers below the radar. Instead, another son of a single parent, rapper 50 Cent, a former drug dealer turned music entrepreneur, gets considerably more acclaim when, after being shot nine times, he resurfaces with an imperial gangsta-rap music career, shattering hip-hop records. He's further validated as a savvy businessman when the May 2007 sale of Vitamin Water, a product he owns a marginal percentage in, nets him $400 million. His stakes in his record label, fashion line, and concert appearances land him in the pages of *Forbes*, *VIBE*, and *The Source* and on MTV, BET, and a host of entertainment programs. He, not Peebles, becomes a household name, and his survival of a shooting in some drug-dealing retaliation goes down in pop culture lore.

Yes, 2007 was a pivotal year. With the election of the nation's first African American president on the horizon, it was the year before the world changed.

CORPORATE CHANGEOVER, SOCIAL MAKEOVER

Although corporate America has some high-profile African Americans in its executive ranks, it still fudges on recruiting and now retaining black employees. Affirmative action and diversity initiatives have not been as far-reaching as many had hoped. While women of color comprise 17 percent of all managerial staff, one Harvard study says corporate America's commitment to diversity is deplorable at best. Frank Dobbin, professor of sociology in Harvard University's Faculty of Arts and Sciences and author of the study, says, "Most companies have not seen very significant changes. Almost all companies are failing."

Companies' clear failure to achieve diversity undermines bottom lines as big businesses find themselves playing catch-up to smaller, more proactive companies that know how to tap overlooked markets of color. Diversity is no longer a choice, cry diversity researchers, it is now a business essential in an increasingly multihued America. Some diversity managers say this inability to manage and support a changing workforce constitutes a silent state of emergency. Dobbin adds, "As the workforce becomes increasingly diverse, they have to [utilize] white women and people of color because you just don't have enough white men to staff all these jobs."

But many African Americans fed up with the glass ceiling, office politics, and downsizing are leaving the corporate ranks in droves to start their own businesses. The number of black women starting businesses in 2002, the last year the Census Bureau counted, leaped 75 percent from five years prior. Meanwhile, African American men between ages twenty-five and thirty-five are more likely to start their own businesses than any other men in the same age group, but that's a little-known fact. Many black Americans believe the number of black-owned businesses is down. In fact, it's common to hear black people refer to the era of segregation as "the heyday" for African American–owned businesses, pointing to black-owned corner stores, shops, and clubs thriving in urban centers like 1940s Harlem, Bronzeville, and other black enclaves in big cities. Yet the fact remains there are more African American–owned businesses today than ever before in the nation's history.

"There are more black men in jail than in college" is another frequently quoted saying in black America. Usually wielded to underscore the lack of progress among the post–civil rights generations, this alleged statistic charges an outright failure of young adults to take advantage of hard-fought opportunity. But it's a "fact," say critics, that was never true. *What Black Men Think*, a documentary by Janks Morton, who says he was "disgusted with the misrepresentations of black men," proves so. Using Census and other government data, Morton debunks the commonly held belief that there are more black men in prison than in college and shows that, in fact, among black men between the ages of eighteen and twenty-five, there is a four-to-one ratio of those in college to those who are incarcerated. But the jail statistic is so ingrained in the speeches of educators, politicians, and activists that it doesn't die. When the Census Bureau later states that more blacks and Latinos live in jails than in college dorms, it makes no mention of the number of commuter students who do not live in dorms, nor does it explain that people in prison are typically twenty-five and older—well past "college dorm" age. Yet the misleading stat is reported by the Associated Press and fed across the world. It's scrolled as a news tag on CNN.

Psychologist and journalist Michael Strambler explores the debate in the *Baltimore Sun*: "The best evidence thus indicates that as a whole, there are more black men in jail and prison than in college—but there are more college-age black men in college than in jail and prison. It doesn't make for a great sound bite; complex realities rarely do."

Although the high school dropout rate for African American teens in some cities hovers around 50 percent (another disputed statistic), record numbers of African Americans by age twenty-five are high school graduates, and more African Americans attend college than ever. In fact, the percentage of Southern-born blacks entering the collegiate ranks is higher than the percentage of blacks in the region.

Just as the truth behind the growing number of black-owned businesses and the "more black men in prison than in college" line shatters ingrained beliefs, the long-standing role of the traditional church as the common denominator in the black experience and the primary launching pad for activism has also changed. Despite the popularity of reigning activists Reverend Jesse L. Jackson and Reverend Al Sharpton, both descendants of a civil rights legacy born in the church, both established black voices in mainstream media, the black church is no longer the primary launching pad for activism and hasn't been since the civil rights movement. "No longer can the clergy claim to be the primary leader within the African American community," said R. Drew Smith, director of the Public Influence of African American Churches project. The emergence of new community and professional groups as well as black politicians eclipses the smaller percentage of black churches that identify themselves as activist, he said. But these groups can't seem to get press coverage. Even the organizations that spawned the Jena 6 protest found themselves skirted by national media until Jackson and Sharpton got involved.

Regentrification is sweeping American cities. Blighted, underserved, inner-city neighborhoods are the new diamonds in the rough. With suburbanites returning downtown and middle America yearning to live the city life, city planners have found a gold mine in troubled black and Latino neighborhoods. The result is mixed housing at its worst. Million-dollar townhomes are built next door to low-income projects. Mansions sit on the same blocks as crack houses. Subdivisions are built smack-dab in the middle of the 'hood. A Mac store in Harlem opens on the same street as Payless.

But these swank residences aren't just homes to white city dwellers; many black professionals are moving in, too. And in a shared capitalistic moment that transcends race, some ask the same question: *When are the poor black people going to leave?*

Isiah Thomas, first black general manager of the New York Knicks, is charged with sexual harassment by a black, female vice president. He says that for a black man to call a black woman a bitch is "acceptable." Black commentators stay oddly quiet on the matter although just months prior they were in an uproar over original shock jock Don Imus calling a girls' college basketball team "nappy-headed hoes." After a national upheaval targeting big-name corporate sponsors, Imus is swiftly fired, only to be rehired months later. But the collective attack shifts from racist, conservative shock jocks to sexist rappers. Hip-hop, once dubbed the voice of young black America, is packaged by corporate labels and primarily targeted to and purchased by white teens in suburbia and the heartland. Sales peak briefly when Kanye West, conscious-inflected rapper, outsells rap's leading king 50 Cent and grosses millions. But despite hip-hop's enormous popularity across color lines, when BET and other groups hold hip-hop forums to analyze the matter, all the panelists are black.

Meanwhile, the NAACP, the nation's oldest and largest civil rights organization, reveals to BlackAmericaWeb that its average member is sixty years old and that it's launching efforts to recruit younger members. They're not alone. Many civil rights organizations, religious institutions, and cultural icons find themselves at the apex of a state of emergency. New and younger members are not signing up. Is it angst? Are people revolting against the very organizations that preserved their freedoms? Not exactly. Some say the organizations no longer speak to their issues. Others say they tried in vain to work with longstanding institutions but were pushed out. Why? No one wanted to hear what they had to say.

But the NAACP, in continued efforts to maintain justice, launches a protest of the rap world's and pop culture's flagrant "culture of disrespect" and has a public funeral for the *n*-word. Oddly, the *n*-word is no longer limited to the confines of racist dialogue and double entendre blackspeak. In part because of hip-hop's global spread, in part because of the word's frequent use in quieter circles, it has emerged on the pop scene as a cool word with "bite." People of all races say the lyrics with no remorse. Rappers performing for white audiences shout "all my niggas put their hands in the air," and the crowd throws their hands up in sheer glee. Some African Americans are offended not by the use of the *n*-word but by the effort to eradicate it. Then iconic rapper Nas unveils the name of his next CD: *Nigger*.

And that's just what we heard on CNN.

Then Barack Obama wins the presidential primaries in Iowa, and everyone's mouth falls open. Within a year, he snatches the Democratic nomination and leapfrogs over centuries of pessimism to become the first African American president of the United States. After Obama gets slammed for having little global political experience during much of the campaign, less than a week after his historic victory, political pundits debate whether the January 2009 inauguration could be moved up some weeks to usher the man in ASAP with hopes of resuscitating an economy whose real estate and stock market backbones had been crippled by lack of federal and corporate oversight.

Simply put, things have changed. Obama manifests much of that change, but the irons were in the fire for over a decade.

There are new dynamics redefining African American life. This book is about that change. Blink and you'll be two steps behind. But how they've changed, for the worse or for the better, to whom and how, depends on which side of the African American ideological fence you're betting on. Politicians, organizations, business leaders, social advocates, average citizens, and the like are heavily vested in the perception of who African Americans *used* to be. How we were defined fifty, twenty-five, even ten years ago. There are those invested in who we *should* be. But there's very little understanding of who we *are*.

I like to think of this dated perception as a one-size-fits-all marketing box, selling the image of African American people in consumer-sized tidbits—easily digestible, perfectly predictable, and satisfying every time.

But that's not the whole picture. This book is about who we are becoming. It's about populations with viewpoints that can't be ignored. This book is about the collective consciousness that would rather ignore change than embrace it. This book is about the new diversity in a community that prides itself on self-definition.

Post Black is about emerging groups, both vibrant and forceful, whose voices and issues are entrenched in communities but are not a part of the social agenda, public discussion, national politics, or collective black identity.

I like to call these untapped groups "the seen but unseen." People's reactions to them are much like the responses to those fictional African Americans living in China (if they are indeed fictitious—I still haven't looked into it). Even though some may admit to their existence, an unusually high number don't know what to make of them. Others are oddly tight-lipped about their place in the African American schemata. Although these emerging groups are strongly rooted culturally, with documented roots in previous generations, their very existence seems to confuse those hell-bent on a monolithic view of the black community.

They are newbies, with different ideals, a variety of lifestyles, and interests that go unnoticed, untapped, and unwanted by the so-called defenders of black identity, because in shifting the paradigm, they shift the power. The ignored groups include but aren't limited to

- *Young black professionals*: "We're like Bigfoot; some have seen us, most doubt we exist," a thirty-one-year-old attorney remarked snidely. Some 17 percent of African Americans have college degrees, with a little over half falling into the under-forty age bracket. This highly sought after group is recognized by high-profile corporations, who target them with luxury-brand items, liquors, and services. Yet they are the group missing from the ranks of established civil rights organizations, churches, and religious groups. At the same time, this demographic has a savvy networking base of professional groups, alumni organizations, and social outlets as well as their own Internet-based media. They have a largely entrepreneurial spirit and are highly educated. But it's a lively world rarely discussed by black America and virtually absent from mainstream coverage.

- *African and Caribbean immigrants*: Over fifty thousand new African immigrants enter the United States legally each year. Large populations from Nigeria, Ghana, and more recently Ethiopia and Somalia are redefining what it means to be African American—an identity typically rooted in a shared history of slavery. Their presence highlights the complexity of the issue of affirmative action and other initiatives designed to redress slavery. Collectively, these immigrant groups send hundreds of millions of dollars back to family in their homelands, redressing centuries of Western-world colonialism. Many are self-employed. "Basically, people are coming to reclaim the wealth that was taken from their countries," Howard Dobson, director of the Schomburg Center for Research in Black Culture, told the *New York Times*.

- *Alternative Christians/non-Christians*: Traditional Christianity is no longer the core religious belief of many African Americans. With a growing number of blacks adopting new expressions of spirituality, the use of fire and brimstone as a common-denominator solution for black salvation and political unity falls on deaf ears. While the influence of the Black Muslims continues, many people are exploring other beliefs including Eastern, African, and Native religions or creating some hybrid mix of many. For many the phrase "I am spiritual" has replaced their affiliation with traditional denominations.

- *The gay, lesbian, bisexual, and transgender community*: This increasingly vocal diverse community's policies and concerns are not intricately etched into discussions about black life. Black GLBTs are largely ignored by black media despite their prevalence in the black community. The military code "don't ask, don't tell" could very well describe the attitudes of traditionalists toward their brothers and sisters of other sexual identities.

- *Biracial/multiracial Americans*: Biracial and multiracial Americans of African American heritage have existed since the first Africans came to the nation's coast. But a new conversation is on the horizon. Many biracial Americans can comfortably embrace two identities, whereas previous racial attitudes maintained the "one-drop rule," forcing biracial people to acknowledge only one. Although changing racial attitudes allow some freedom in their identity, many biracial adults struggle to embrace one ethnicity over the other.

- *Community-based artists*: Historically revered as change agents intricately linked to social movements, underground and fine artists may have been marginalized in the media by the culture's obsession with pop stardom, but their impact has not been. In fact, the culture of black artists including poets, actors, painters, dancers, singers, and more may be larger than in previous decades. But the role of these artists in the midst of streamlined corporate values has yet to be defined. Debate also rages over the responsibility black pop stars have to the community. Some argue that, with the world as their stage, they are the culture's most underutilized ambassadors.

Rarely are these groups and their unique issues expressed fully in the policies and organizations addressing African American decision makers. In many cases there is a fundamental resistance to doing so. But to do something about the divide is to acknowledge the divide. Like all responsible soothsayers, once you acknowledge it, then you have to do something about it. Something radically different. While to do the same thing and expect different results is insanity by most people's standards, to blindly ignore change and keep up the old fight is disastrous.

Which leads to other questions: Who benefits by ignoring change? Who benefits by rotating the same incorrect stats on the dire state of black America over and over again, and how does this misinformation affect African American teens in their quest for identity? Conversation about the dynamics of a black working class becomes increasingly complicated if you acknowledge that a large contingent of young black professionals is emerging from HBCUs and state and Ivy League schools. Can the black church continue to be a political launching pad if you acknowledge that a growing number of African Americans don't go to church, aren't traditional Christians, and may not be Christian at all? How can traditional black organizations begin to openly acknowledge their gay, lesbian, and bisexual African American constituency when, in walking a line to appease conservative Christians and radical thinkers, they stay silent on the issue? How can the black agenda incorporate people who are as white, Mexican, Japanese, or Indian as they are black—and proud of it?

How does a political candidate understand that the ranks of new black business owners he's reaching out to don't have storefronts in black neighborhoods? Can an artist be black without doing "black art"—an array of figurative or historical images reflecting the black experience? While fans are urging rap and R & B artists to be social justice leaders, can these artists really advocate for change in a pop culture fueled by fantasy and the bottom line? How do you incorporate the histories of new African immigrants into the new black consciousness when most African Americans' relationship to Africa is nostalgic at best?

"I, Too, Sing America" was Langston Hughes's groundbreaking poem—an affirmation that the darker brother has rights to America's fruits and labor, too. A phrase that embodies the death-defying actions that compelled the nation to radically rethink its policies on race and economics, rethink its history, rethink its identity, and rethink it fast or face a national upheaval.

I, too, am African American. It's not exactly a war-torn battle cry. It wasn't the leading sentiment in the civil rights movement, nor was it a statement that brought the nation to war with itself. But it does reflect the seedlings of another simmering uprising within the African American community as it's forced to redefine itself or face cultural implosion. *I, too, am African American* defines the changing landscape of today's African American population—and includes those who don't fit into the nation's collective definition of itself, who don't fit into the African American regime's idea of itself, who aren't represented by politicians or preachers, don't match the hip-hop–inflected media stereotypes nor the enhanced images of ridiculous wealth, stupendous crimes, or destitute poverty flashed on the evening news. They are a new breed with different ideals and a variety of lifestyles and interests that go unnoticed, untapped, and unwanted by the so-called defenders of black identity because, in shifting the paradigm, these outliers shift the power to define what being African American truly is.

Much is at stake. It's evident that longstanding approaches and policies designed to address the concerns of African Americans need a serious overhaul. New people need to come to the table.

Without some resolve, an opportunity to build on the diversity within this community could be lost. Longstanding institutions could vanish, their policies rendered ineffective. And the power of the African American collective, both economically and politically, that's been leveraged to force the nation's hand at fairness in the past could be jeopardized.

This book presents a case for identity. Historically, African American life has been rich in this question of who we are. The power to define was snuffed out and flatlined with the African holocaust and Jim Crow and reclaimed through the vigilant fights against them. Deciphering negative versus positive images and who's real and who isn't while combating a history of racist stereotypes is a perpetual dilemma. It shadows the debate over authenticity versus inclusiveness. As black identity moved from ideology to bankable business, experts surfaced, vested interests grew, and some groups got shut out.

Questions of identity arise whenever a person identifies him- or herself as black in America. I'm sure other ethnic groups wrestle with this, too, just as most people explore individual identity and the way self-expression alters their lives. However, because identity is so ingrained in African American culture and history, I felt it was necessary to revisit. As you read through these pages, I hope you will absorb these looks at the "seen but unseen," because they are African American, too.

1

THE GENERATION GAP
THE YOUNG BLACK PROFESSIONAL

Members of the baby boomer, X, and Y generations wrestle to merge ideals and systems.

My dad doesn't think I have a job.

He's never said this, of course. He reads my stories on people he's never heard of in the Gen X and Y mags he wouldn't be reading without my byline. He's been to the movie premieres in chic places he wouldn't normally attend packed with the ghosts of futures present, aka the "invisibles"—the array of professional and artist types of color he's heard about via word of mouth, à la my word of mouth. The ones he's heard are moving into Chicago's old "low end," now Bronzeville, turning crack houses into quarter-mil condos.

These invisibles do things in the even more invisible world known as the Internet, where they find news that's not on the nightly six o'clock broadcast or in the paper. Where they send little messages called e-mails and texts, galvanizing more of our ilk to bond over issues that could easily be discussed in a phone conversation.

My dad doesn't believe in the Internet. Nor is he an advocate of cell phones, preferring to bag a bunch of quarters for those rare pay phones that have survived the cell phone takeover. Since computers haven't gone the way of the eight-track, he's resigned himself to be forever "old school."

My dad's an interesting guy. Born and raised in a small town in Texas, he is proud to be an old-school grad of Prairie View A&M. He was baptized in civil rights and wears the looming crown of justice, a ten-gallon cowboy hat that signals "I'm taking names and kicking butt" or "black cowboys live" or "I'm a federal investigator with the United States of America." He's a political news junkie and horse rider. Reads the *Sun-Times* and *Jet*. He's got a storehouse of collectibles from his heroes: a poster of boxing's first black heavyweight champion, Jack Johnson; a picture of himself with Muhammad Ali; JESSE JACKSON FOR PRESIDENT buttons; and, more recently, a Barack

Obama T-shirt my brother gave him for Father's Day.

As for hip-hop, to him it's a foreign aberration where kids twist their fingers in funny ways and spit indiscernible words to beats that resemble a train wreck in some space-age effort to highjack the *real* music that should be on the radio: James Brown, Otis Redding, and maybe a little Aretha.

As a kid during the house music versus rap war in Chicago, I asked Dad which of the roaring new school sounds he preferred. "That's like asking would I rather be shot or stabbed," he replied with a smile. The only rap song I remember him liking when I was growing up was "I Go to Work" by Kool Moe Dee, for obvious reasons.

A stickler for tradition, Dad usually meets me on a Sunday around the same time at the same restaurant. We changed restaurants only recently because his favorite place—a lonely, black-owned soul food diner across the street from the Regal Theater on Seventy-Ninth Street with no sign, never more than two customers, and a jukebox full of blues bootlegs—closed unexpectedly. So now we meet at a Hyde Park sports bar with a couple of pool tables and a bowling alley. We meet at one of two tables, one indoor, the other outdoor. Nevertheless, you can see his Clint Eastwood strut a mile away, and when we meet for lunch I always get a kick out of his perspective on life.

I should have known change was on the horizon when he made an unexpected comment about rapper 50 Cent. "I think he's finally starting to understand more about manhood," he remarked. I did a double take. Was my father talking about a rapper? My sister, who had joined us on this day, and I looked at one another. "Tell us more, Dad." And he went on about boys turning into men, understanding what's important in life. He made some analogy about young buffaloes and old buffaloes.

He retired recently. Now that Obama is president, impossible is possible. Hell has frozen over, so to speak, and thanks to my taking him around to a few of my own haunts, he's content that the world's not going to hell in a handbasket and that it is officially safe for him to retire. He can tuck the six-shooter away. There are apparently others who can now take the reins, he remarked, after recognizing that there were people in my demographic who were doing things with their lives, even if it didn't make a heap of sense.

While my dad would joke that he didn't have anything to say to anyone under fifty at his job and prided himself on being the youngest member of his all-black service organization, he was never opposed to progress. Opposed to technology, perhaps, but never progress. He was highly disappointed in peers of his generation who made disparaging remarks about Obama (before it became totally uncool to do so). "If you can't get excited about this," he said of Obama's presidential bid, "you can't get excited about anything."

Generation gaps don't begin with the advent of hip-hop. I ran across a quote from a literary great who took serious issue with the "new generations of erudite drunkards" in the 1400s. My mom, a Chicago-born daughter of the 1960s and social advocate who spent all of her professional career in educational administration, frequently talks of her own father, a classically trained musician whose world went topsy-turvy with the onslaught of civil rights and the Black Power movement. He couldn't get past the Afros, the brazen pride in the naturally tight curls he'd been taught should be straightened with Murray's grease. He couldn't stand them, she said. Nor was my grandfather a fan of the blues or its rock and rhythm-and-blues derivatives. "It's too repetitive," he'd say. "All that ooh, baby, baby, ooh, baby, baby. How many times is he going to say it?" He wouldn't let my mom march with King when he came to Chicago. King, in his mind, was a young, eloquent rabble-rouser kicking dust on their northern, middle-class convictions. "To think, today, King has a holiday. My father wouldn't know how to take that," Mom said, laughing. But even he knew times were changing. He was fascinated by humans' foray into space. As for earthly matters, my mother convinced him to go against the notorious political machine and vote for comic/activist Dick Gregory for mayor. In 1968, my grandfather passed away, a decision, my mom often says, that he made because the world flip to come was too radical for him. On the other hand, her mom, a Mississippi-born beauty and daughter of self-sufficient landowners, was all for this new world. As fashions and conventions turned the corner over the next few decades, so did my grandmother. Change was a part of life, she reasoned. She passed away before the turn of the next century.

TELLTALE SIGNS

When you're taught to give back, it's usually recommended that you start by working with an organization that served as your rock during childhood. After college I became reaffiliated with one organization in particular—the one that had the greatest impact on my character development. As often happens in childhood, I took for granted the values instilled in me there, and I didn't realize how rare these nuggets of inspiration were and how much I valued the lessons I'd learned until I entered the real world. For the sake of my own growth, I continued my affiliation with the organization and when asked would volunteer and do workshops for kids. For the sake of anonymity, I'll call this organization the Institution. The Institution, like many longstanding black organizations, was founded by one of those battle-worn geniuses whose model for success survived racism, political games, and the changing of the guards. The Institution was a pioneer in an area in which few had tread and had been bucking the system miles ahead of the curve for so long that ideologies it implemented in the 1970s were just hitting the mainstream post-2K. But half a century after its creation, for some reason no one could fully explain, the Institution was unusually heavy with longtime members and light on both new and younger recruits. Nearly three-quarters of its members were over fifty-five. A handful of seasoned members warned the heedless few that the Institution was approaching a crisis if it didn't do something immediately. Hoping to make a difference, a few twenty- and thirtysomethings who aimed to boost the young adult membership launched a good-natured auxiliary group I'll call the Firm. The Firm's mission was to create programs for the Gen X and Gen Y demo, to keep this group enthusiastic about the Institution's mission, and to support this crew of invisibles as they took on larger responsibilities within the organization. I was recruited to join the Firm. It got off to a good start. It comprised a group of professionals, most with bachelor's and postgraduate degrees—a round table including some down-to-earth physicians, engineers, artists, real estate agents, educators, and students. After a few feel-good social events got the group excited, the membership decided to create a series of workshops to attract new members to the Firm and to service the Institution at large. Well-written, fully financed proposals with all the i's dotted and t's crossed were created and proudly presented to the Institution. None of them were approved.

The problem: the proposals were too good, the Firm's membership was too eager, and the Institute's leadership frowned upon these new faces whose knowledge and vigor challenged their sedentary conventions. The Firm's talent and goodwill drew a line in the sand. *Who the hell do these kids think they are?* stormed the Institute leaders.

So instead of approving anything, the Institution hit the Firm with a list of requirements, a few hoops to jump through if they wanted to be fully recognized as, well, adults. A little miffed, the Firm members nonetheless agreed, completed the required "course work" so they'd be taken seriously, and began cultivating new proposals. The organization needed, among other things, more community outreach, marketing, relevant programs, and revenue streams, and proposal after proposal created events and programs to address all of these. After some serious campaigning a few proposals saw the light of day, but it soon became obvious that the Institution's leadership and its dire plea for new blood was all talk. The key leadership had no interest in the Firm's mission. They didn't want any smart, educated, energetic young people with a bag full of new-wave ideas and notions of helping or being future leaders. Stop writing proposals and go stuff some envelopes.

The situation was totally bizarre. The Institution countered the Firm's success by banning it from promoting itself either internally or externally. If Firm members did anything as a group outside of the Institution, they could not use the Institution's name or that of the auxiliary itself. Even when a few events were approved, the Institution usurped all major decisions by claiming that the members were "too young" and "didn't know what they were doing" and undermined the events' success by pulling budgets, axing promotion, and targeting Firm members for exile. Yes, I said exile. Hurt by this widespread rejection from the people they had grown up admiring, many in the Firm just left. They would "serve" elsewhere or wouldn't serve at all. But the greater calamity was that the Firm was merely trying to help. Not a single soul in that group had any grand dreams of storming the Institution and assuming leadership. Their lives were busy enough without running a multimillion-dollar service organization as a latter-day side hustle. But eventually the

Institution's fanatical resistance compelled many in the Firm to aim for leadership. The remaining Firm diehards aimed to prove that Firm members were in fact intelligent people with valuable talents that could turn the Institution around if the leaders took off their stuck-on stupid hats and listened. And that morphed into wanting to save the Institution itself, because the members' behavior and "let's rid ourselves of these willful youth" antics undermined not just the Firm but the lifeline of the Institution itself. The die-hard Firm members became vigilant, countering efforts of annihilation— yes, I said annihilation—with some minor victories that went unacknowledged. Battle axe in hand, some of these vigilantes wound up chopping their way up the ladder, moving into other auxiliaries, and taking on larger leadership roles. But no matter how high they rose or what roles they took on, disillusionment was inevitable.

And nearly all at various points seriously considered leaving and forming a new Institution run by none other than the Firm members themselves.

In the Institution's defense, there were many innovative old-schoolers who advocated for the Firm. They weren't very loud about it, preoccupied with their own battles, but they outnumbered the core leadership and tried in their quiet way to support us. One such event was a panel held by one of the auxiliaries. Leaders rounded up a few articulate Gen Xers with nothing in common other than their loose affiliation with the Institution and a few framed diplomas and asked us to talk about how we came to exist. They looked at us like we were talking pandas, their mouths agape as they tried to ask well-intentioned questions that were as disparate as east and west. Always one to advocate for clarity, I just asked the audience point-blank, "What issues do you have with young adults? What is it you don't like about us?" They were quiet at first. But the hands came up slowly.

"We don't like the way you dress," one fiftyish woman uttered quietly. Mind you, everyone on the panel was suited up. But the audience echoed her disdain. If I were to find the common denominator for all their concerns, it centered around this fact that they just didn't like the way we dressed. Those saggy, baggy jeans with the tightie whities and boxers playing peek-a-boo were just the tip of the iceberg. We, as in all young black people, dressed entirely too casual at work. We wore sandals when we should wear closed-toed shoes. Some of us didn't wear pantyhose at all, just our bare legs and a pair of pumps, they said. Too many women wore suit jackets that hugged their curves instead hiding their waist, or sundresses. Some even wore tops with no sleeves! Young men sported button-ups and refused to tuck them into their pants. And sometimes they wore suit jackets with creaseless jeans. And what's up, they asked, with wearing white in the winter? One young panelist appalled by the superficial nature of it all finally quipped, "It's not like everyone over forty is well dressed. Some of y'all are tacky, too." But his outrage fell on deaf ears. The audience continued its rant. A few people copped to the fact that they at one time wore bell-bottoms and micro-minis. Then the discussion morphed into an audience agreement that how young people dressed was secondary to the reality that we have a level of freedom about the way we dress that some were puzzled by and others were jealous of but all found very discomfiting to their way of life. This fashion obsession as the focal point of our intergenerational conversation was, by my standards, very weird. I think the other panelists and I silently agreed to a code of silence on the matter.

But this fight-for-change thing took on new dimensions as the Institution's peril reached civil war levels. *What were we fighting for?* became the philosophical question of the day. Soon, the Firm members who remained wound up fighting less for the validity of the

Firm than for the Institution's mission itself. Death wasn't going to come, as some had predicted, solely because of the absence of young members but rather because of what young members symbolize—change and innovation, which can come from people of all ages and backgrounds. The key Institution leaders, in their attempts to thwart innovation and protect their own fiefdoms, left a nice little vortex for a group of pirates—some power-hungry, extremist baby boomers who didn't give a flying fig about the Institution's mission and I think had a chip or two on their shoulders against the great generation. The great generation didn't give up its power fast enough, these boomers reasoned, and now you have these over-eager Gen X and Yers with their dastardly Internet thinking—they're going to slip in and take my piece of the pie, like that Obama guy. We'll show them, they said. Dollar bills danced in their eyes as they bear-hugged the Institution's prestige and treasure. Cash was king, and the pirates were uniformly aligned: the Institution should become a circus.

Yes, a circus.

Those members of the Firm who were left and weren't battle-weary joined their once quiet but now vocal baby boomer and great generation supporters and became part of la Résistance de Circus. Even some of the Johnny-come-lately leadership joined la Résistance de Circus, but I couldn't help thinking that all of this could have been avoided. Because it could have been avoided. Enter la Fiasco.

Now if this had been the first time I'd witnessed la Fiasco up close and personal, I could trump it up to plain old politics. But I'd witnessed la Fiasco at least two or three times before. La Fiasco was not an isolated incident. The Institution symbolized what was happening on smaller and larger scales in countless well-meaning institutions that were hallmarks in black communities. Frankly, it's not a dynamic limited to black institutions, either, but it serves as a marker for changing dynamics everywhere.

There was a generational jealousy among some black baby boomers. Not among all, but enough for it to become an issue. A baby boomer writer I ran across spelled it out in an essay. This hip-hop generation is arrogant. They have no respect for their elders, she wrote. Well, that charge isn't a new one. But she continued rattling off all the opportunities we have, the access to education, the ability to pursue dreams she couldn't have dreamed of at our age. I thought she was going to say that we didn't take advantage of our opportunities. I'd heard that complaint before, and sure, there are people who could do some stepping up. But her anger stemmed not from our failure to take advantage of these opportunities but from the fact that we *did* take advantage of them, flashing our fancy trinkets and possessions, walking around with optimism, thinking we were somebody. We, as in me and my cronies, hadn't so much as marched for anything, our rights had been served to us on a silver platter, and we had the audacity to succeed, she said.

Shouldn't she be happy? I thought. Apparently not. She had an issue because we weren't loyal. *Loyal to what?* I wondered. She was angry that we had opportunities at our age that she hadn't, and here she was, despite her achievements, still trying to claw her way up the ladder while we, as in this Gen X and Y group, seemingly leaped ahead. We were moving too fast for our own good and needed to be stopped. Now, she didn't write that last line, but she might as well have.

My college friend Regina and I discussed it once. "It's like when I would go to some of those journalist conventions," she said. "Some of the people really wanted to help, but others acted like you were trying to take their job." I've been fortunate to have many baby boomer advisers come into my life and guide me appropriately. Several have dedicated their lives to aiding as many young prospects as possible with the clear instruction that we're to do the same. That's how we pay them back. And they are never anyone you would expect or seek out. Everyone I actually asked to mentor me said no. On the other hand, there are these baby boomer angels, age-defying life coaches with a zest for life and an eye for molding, who will come sweeping into your life like parental superheroes always telling you to screw what everyone else says and just do it. You have everything you need, they'll say. They hop from one talent in the rough to the next, dosing their wisdom before their enemy, the baby boomer hate brigade, takes hold.

The quest for a mentor often falls flat with many Gen Xers and Yers trying to come up in the world, a fact reiterated when I interviewed an assortment of accomplished professionals and asked them if they had mentors. None of them did, but they were all part of young professional groups that helped facilitate networks and information. This was nice, I thought, but how much invaluable experience was lost due to the fact that so many Gen Xers and Yers are limited to networks with their own peers? All made reference to the baby boomer angel, some person, usually in another field, who gave them the advice of their lives before zapping back into superhero land.

Naturally, everyone grows out of the mentor phase at some point, but people positioning themselves as gatekeepers to success under the guise of mentorship can be the carrot dangling before fast risers who are moving a little *too* quick for their baby boomer contemporaries. *He's too young for this job. . . . She needs to be trained. . . . They need to be mentored.* If I've heard it once I've heard it a thousand times, and it's always said by someone in the baby boomer hater parade who sees a glimmer of promise in some younger person's eyes that they don't see in their own.

YIN AND YANG: GEN X AND GEN Y

My younger sister, Veronica, is the socially traditional Tweedledee to my lefty Tweedledum. We're two different sides of the seesaw, so to speak. While my inquisitiveness led me to the writer's life via journalism and film, she hones her keen mind through the study of social psychology. She's embarked on postgrad studies at Howard University in Washington, D.C., and when she comes back to Chicago she's got an attaché case of theories to test.

"You're very Gen X," she said to me recently. Gen X includes people who were born somewhere between 1965 and 1980. She, born post-1980, was a Gen Yer, aka a millennial, and based on her research into the generational divide, while we both grew up in the same household and had the same parents and the same education, our takes on life were different.

I hadn't heard the take on Gen X from a Gen Yer before, and I figured my sister's insights should be interesting.

"Your generation is attracted to entrepreneurial activities where you are in control," she said with the authority of a professor. "You aren't into group activities. You want a boss who can tell you what the end product is so you can create the plan instead of being given the plan. You tend to question what people tell you. A lot of times that can be related to low voter turnout when you guys were younger, because you questioned things going on. Gen X is in such a solitary mode."

It didn't sound so bad to me. So I asked for more.

"And how is Gen Y so different?" I asked, having some inkling that Gen Y would be described as all rainbows and fig leaves compared to my generation, a medley of former forty-ounce beer drinkers with an affinity for oversized jeans.

"We're the ideal," she answered. "Generation Y is very, very collaborative. Very group-oriented, very optimistic, and very bold. We really like feedback and support. We like a little bit of leeway so we can be creative. But we need the pat on the back and to have someone hold our hand along the way to know that we are doing a good job. Instead of getting irritated and leaving the system as a whole, like you guys, the Gen Y are like, 'We're going to work together until we get this right.' We do this because of the relationship we had with our parents when we were younger." She explained how Gen Yers were part of the decision-making process at home. "Our parents talked to us more. Not that we were on the same level, but they asked 'What do you think?' 'Where do you want to go?' 'Do you want to go to Disneyland or Disney World?' So when we get into the work world we feel we are more about negotiation.

"You guys just opted out," she claimed. "X is like, 'I'm going to do my own thing because I have valid ideas,' whereas Y is like, 'I have my own ideas, and I'm going to be heard because my parents listened to me.'" I thought about it. My sister *did* feel she had unusually high leverage for negotiation in her work environment, especially considering she was an intern. On the other hand, I hadn't worked exclusively for one company in some years, and certainly not in an office. Maybe she had a point.

"You guys didn't have the whole coddling experience," she said.

"Really?" I asked.

"We want to be a part of the system, you guys don't. On the other hand, if Gen Xers see they can't do it on their own and realize, 'Oh, benefits are a good idea,' and they come into the establishment, it's like they lost a little bit of themselves or like, 'Great, now I'm back in the system I don't believe in.' But that part's just my hypothesis."

I thought about my colleagues and friends, most of whom had some entrepreneurial endeavor or at least dreamed of one.

"Gen X will look at Y and will say they are bratty and needy," she added.

"That's not just a sibling thing?" I joked.

"Uh, no. We're always looking for feedback. Gen X doesn't necessarily dislike feedback, but you don't *need* it. Gen Y feels we are special just for who we are. If we get an A, great, if we get a C, great. *We* have other qualities that make us feel good, like we're a good friend or a good listener. We feel this way," she claimed, "because of the abundance of cartoons we had, like Barney—we're special regardless. My generation was on a lot of teams, but it wasn't about the competition, it was about everyone doing good, everyone is a winner. So the level of competition that my generation feels with each other isn't the same. For the baby boomers," she went on, "it's like you're a winner or a loser. For Gen X, you're a winner or a slacker, and you're going to be the best winner or slacker you can be. Whereas with Y, it's like, we're all good in our own way. Plus we're very good at multitasking and managing our time. The success of Barack has been attributed to Gen Y. You guys, at least when you were younger, were too pessimistic to vote."

"Are you sure there's no bias here?" I asked.

"This is all based on research," she asserted.

For the first time ever, Veronica said, you had the baby boomers, Gen X, and Gen Y, which was causing some very serious multigenerational dynamics that diversity managers were trying to take the lead on.

"The baby boomers are staying in their jobs longer because they don't want to retire, unlike the traditionalists, who worked to live and wanted to retire. Baby boomers tend to be in positions that they like and tend to work longer. The baby boomers initially wanted everyone to do T-ball activities and group activities," she said, "but they saw that Gen Xers weren't down for all that. That's the way it's been for a good fifteen, twenty years. Gen Y comes in, and they are totally throwing things off. Gen Yers are the ideal candidates because they are so bright-eyed and bushy tailed, but managers were so used to you solitary Gen X types. Gen X is like, 'What's up with all the conversation? Just give me the product.' But Gen Y is like, 'Let's talk about it. Do you like this? Do you like that?' Gen Y is a little more sensitive because they're used to people catering to them. Whereas Gen X is like, 'No one will listen to me, we'll just do it on our own.'"

"So how am I typical Gen X?" I asked, returning to her initial point.

"I think you fall into it because you kind of do the whole 'I'm going to have my own business, be my own boss' type of attitude— at least that fueled most of your endeavors," she answered. "I think you're a bit cynical about certain establishments and have an attitude of 'If I don't do it, it won't get done. I have to go hard, and if I have to be tough, that's fine as long as it gives me the outcome I desire.'"

I thought of all those "we ain't goin' nowhere, get rich or die trying" anthems in the hip-hop world that were the soundtrack to the Gen X edict.

"I think that getting feedback and a thumbs-up is not completely necessary for you to do what you're doing. It may not faze you either way. Once you see what you want, you're going to go for it. If somebody likes it, cool, but if they don't, it doesn't matter because you're going to do it anyway. Once you do find a person who you believe in," she went on, "who is confident, who's not shucking and jiving, it is a person you respect. I don't think your generation respects a lot of people. Not that you're disrespectful, but when you find them your level of respect is so high because you don't let anyone into your little bubble. It probably brings more substance to your relationships because your values are so high, whereas Gen Y is like, 'Everybody is supposed to like me.'"

But my sister kept weaving this Gen X-as-cynics story that I disagreed with, and I told her so.

"I wouldn't call myself cynical," I said.

"No, you're cynical," she quipped. "I see it. Even if you're talking about an observation you have, you may say what you actually saw, then your next comment is 'But I think this is what they really meant, and I don't believe them.' That's kind of your MO. I don't know if that's the journalist in you or if that's just your generation. You have a chipper tone but beneath all that there's cynicism. You don't believe in people."

"I do believe in people," I retorted.

"No, you don't. In the back of your mind you feel that if that person messes up you're going to be able to get it done anyway. If you constantly have a plan D, a plan ABCD in mind, it means you don't trust what people say they are going to do. If you're constantly making decisions in that way, it's rooted in total cynicism."

If there was cynicism, it was certainly based on eager efforts to work within systems that fell through, I thought.

"And how are you different?" I asked.

"Being around you has given me an edge. It could be a Chicago thing, too. That could be a Midwestern, squint your eyes, 'I don't believe what you have to bring to the game' attitude. To an extent I have that, too," she admitted. "But in my mind if a person says they're going to do it, they're going to do it. I think I listen to the person, if it makes sense and they seem happy about what they're saying, then I trust them. I feel the vibe. I ask the questions that I need to ask. Not to make my generation seem stupid, we may ask three questions, but if they answer then we let them in. But with you all, it's a subtle interrogation over the course of months. It's a different motivation."

"So what's the upside of Gen X?" I asked.

"The whole driven deal. You all are very accountable for your actions. You think, 'If I don't make it, it's because I didn't do this or I didn't do this.' You can't blame it on the system, because you're not a part of it. It's a kind of accountability that other generations don't have, 'cause you guys are like, 'We're out.' I think this can lead to an entirely different level of pessimism."

"We are not pessimists," I said. Why do they always say Gen Xers are pessimists?

"Well maybe you're not a total pessimist, but think about your peers who were born between, say, '65 and '72," she said.

A few ambitious, noteworthy cynics came to mind. Again, I think she had a point.

"I believe y'all were already a little critical in high school," she added. "In college, when you got more information about the real deal and then had your ideas validated by college professors, who are a little left of center anyway, it just made it stick. Then you get to the work force, where there are all these social hierarchies, and you leave and do the entrepreneurial thing. I think every Gen X person has done something entrepreneurial," she went on, "but doing your own thing is hard knocks, especially when you act like there hasn't ever been a template for it. If that entrepreneurial venture takes off, you're going to be hard on the Gen Y people, you're going to be like, 'I created this myself, I did this myself,' and Gen Y will tell you to chill out." Then she pondered again.

"Gen X will be these tough, hard-knock bosses," she added.

"What?"

"I think when you get to the top you'll be worse than the baby boomers. Because it's a real no-tolerance type of deal. At least with the traditionalists, like Grandma and them, they had a heart because they were preoccupied with families," she said. "But you guys aren't having kids, either, so the whole paternal/maternal instinct isn't there. You'll be fine with people working under you doing their own thing as long as they give you the product you want, but you can't tolerate the whining. You're like, 'Why are you talking to me? Why are you in my face?' You have no tolerance for excuses either. Just look at Puffy," she said, referring to his *Making the Band* drama. "They give the underdogs a chance to get in, but if they don't make the bar by a certain time, they gotta go. I think the level of empathy is a bit low with you guys."

I started to giggle. My sister continued.

"But I also believe that Gen Yers tend to warm that mean, cold heart of the Gen X people, and at some point you will see that humans are humans," she asserted. "Every generation evolves. So after being cynical jerks for substantial parts of your lives, you'll hear Gen Y say, 'Smell the roses while you can. We can be friends and don't have to be competitive.'"

Her critiques of Gen X were uncannily similar to those Gen X critiques of the baby boomers. Funny.

"So you wouldn't want to work for me?" I asked. She paused and thought about it.

"I wouldn't mind working for you in that you're a young person who looks like me, who has creative ideas, and is driven. But I think it may be hard, in that . . . " she paused again and mulled it over. "I like to know routines, what's expected of me. I like to know, 'At this time, you're going to be in this place, and it's going to be on a daily basis.' If that's jumbled a bit, I think it could throw me off."

"So you don't like variety. You *want* a routine?" I asked. Too funny. My whole generation loathed routine.

"I don't have a problem doing different stuff," Veronica objected. "I would just like to know *the day before* what I'm going to do, some type of advance notice. If you ask would I work for you,

I'm like, 'Where would I sit? Where's my office? What's the work environment?' You're cool working from home," she pointed out, "but I'm not cool doing that. I want to go to an office and bounce ideas off people and dress up and have people comment on my outfit. I like the daily workings of an office. Some people like the whole working in pajamas deal, but I would rather work downtown."

I was doubled over in laughter. The working independently piece, which my peers cherished, was tantamount to hell for someone like my sister. This was too funny.

"What's so funny?" she asked. And I kept laughing. "What's so funny?"

THE AFRICAN DIASPORA
NEW IMMIGRANTS IN AFRICAN AMERICA

The recent influx of African immigrants continues to redefine the black experience in America.

Will the real African Americans please rise?

A colleague of mine introduced me to an English journalist. A thirtysomething guy living the backpacker life in the States, he was writing a blog for the *London Mirror* on his cross-country trip across the great U.S. of A. and wanted to talk to me to get some insight into the black experience. After a very lengthy discussion defending how I can be black and not listen to Muddy Waters daily, we wound up discussing the terms "black" and "African American."

"What's the difference?" he asked.

"Some people feel 'African American' has more of a cultural identity," I responded.

He nodded. Then I added a footnote.

"Oh, and it can also refer to blacks with longtime roots in America, versus if your roots are elsewhere."

He took a swig from his Starbucks machiatto and frowned.

"What do you mean?"

"For example, if you're talking about African American culture, that term refers to maybe the experiences of slavery and the culture that emerged afterward."

"Uh-huh."

"Versus if you just immigrated from, say, Nigeria. If you're Nigerian, obviously you're African American in that you're black and live in this country, but culturally, well, at first you may have very strong ties to Nigeria and prefer 'Nigerian American.'"

"But they're still black, right?" he asked, confused.

"Well, yeah, but the culture they emerged from is different. So it just depends on what you're talking about culturally. If you're talking about soul food and blues, you're talking about African American culture. If you're talking about reggae and salt fish, you're talking about Jamaican culture. Of course, you have Jamaicans in

America. You have people whose grandparents were Jamaican, and they eat Jamaican food and partake in Jamaican culture, but they're African American."

"And they'd call themselves Jamaican American?"

"Maybe, it depends," I answered.

"But they're still black and in America?"

"Yeah."

I rehashed the logic a few times, but he was still confused. I acted like his confusion was beyond my comprehension, but in truth intra-ethnic matters always have complex logic when verbalized to other cultures, and I felt like I was experiencing that awkward, eighth-grade moment when my Irish classmate asked why all the black kids were in love with the young black boy for his green eyes.

"There are a lot of white kids with green eyes, and no one thinks they're so hot," she said.

"I know," was all I could mutter, without winding through the details of beauty/color politics.

I thought I'd done a fair job of explaining the difference between "black" and "African American" to my English friend. But a few days later, while I was perusing a secondhand store in Atlanta, I got another call from him.

"Ytasha, I'm working on this story, but I gotta ask you, what's the difference again? Why can't I just say 'black'?"

"'Black' refers to everybody who's black. African American refers specifically to blacks in the United States and sometimes the specific culture. Black encompasses a lot of cultures, and African American is one of those cultures."

The store owner, a young black woman in her thirties, was ear hustling, so I brought her in.

"Do you prefer 'black' or 'African American'?" I asked her.

"African American. I'd like to be connected to a landmass and not a color, thank you," she said tartly.

"See, there you go," I told him, juggling the phone while raising an eyebrow at a 1940s raccoon fur scarf with the head attached.

"Well, how am I supposed to know which blacks are immigrants and which aren't? How am I supposed to know who's African American and who isn't if everybody's black?"

"I don't know. Just use 'African American' to be safe."

"But I thought you said 'black' includes everybody."

"Yeah, it's tricky."

I could have chalked this dialogue up to the ridiculousness of intra-race semantics until I stumbled upon a *New York Times* article on Abdulaziz Kamus, an Ethiopian-born activist in his forties. He was among a cadre of black health experts and community leaders debating how to educate African Americans on the dangers of prostate cancer. When he suggested that they focus some attention on African immigrants he was promptly reminded that the campaign was for "African Americans." Kamus had lived in the United States for twenty years. "What am I supposed to call myself?" he asked.

NOSTALGIA REVISITED

I was in the eighth grade when the term "African American" came into vogue. Jesse Jackson Sr. ushered in our latest upgrade, and no sooner had I heard the term on the nightly news than my white, very liberal, and, I assume, former hippie literature teacher was using it like the new vocabulary word of the day. Jackson and my eighth-grade lit teacher were the only two people I'd ever heard use it. My parents had a death grip on the term "black." They'd shouted it with pride during the "black is beautiful" movement and felt it rang with strength as it reclaimed a new identity and progression. But "African American" had more of a cultural tie, and I began using the word, too.

Growing up, Africa was more of a symbol than a place. The pulsating heart for our lifeline, the pot of gold on the other side of the oppression rainbow, with the generations of slavery so thick no family reunion tree could seem to navigate back to it. If you're lucky, like me, you can go back to at least the last generation or two of slaves before running into their slave-master fathers.

Nevertheless, there's a great deal of nostalgia associated with Africa. Africa is where we came from. It was home. *Roots*, the award-winning miniseries of the 1970s, played like an annual after-school special in the 1980s. Kunta (LeVar Burton) himself, who magically wound up on *Reading Rainbow* while *Roots* was in its marathon run, was a collective symbol for that nameless African ancestor few African Americans with longtime roots in this country knew.

Africa was the place to get back to. But it was too costly for regular trips, and until the recent development of DNA tests that can trace your ancestry, you were limited to some chance info passed on through the years to guide you to a place and a people you could call home. Nevertheless, maintaining ties to Africa symbolically was very important. It came via cultural events, museum visits, book reports, African dance class, and fashion. African medallions, cowry shell necklaces. While my first elementary school's one-way corridor was lined with pictures of black heroes every Black History Month, rarely, if ever, did we learn about any Africans, unless you count those incredibly informative Budweiser African King and Queen posters that popped up in barbershops, Arab-owned grocery stores, and my uncle's basement in the early 1990s.

"Mom," I asked, "how come we don't learn about Africa during Black History Month?" Her response was something like "First things first," as if I had to learn the history of Africans in America before I'd get to study about the golden age of Africa. She was right. High school and elementary school focused heavily on African American history, and college opened the doors to Africa.

In my Topics in Africa class, I had to memorize all the countries in Africa and identify them on a map. We were introduced to various cultures and histories. My professor came from the Democratic Republic of the Congo, which at the time was still Zaire, and he talked about coming to America for school and being told by his white counterparts to stay away from African Americans, particularly African American women, who, he was told, only wanted his money. He said he passed himself off as royalty, hoping that would make him more intriguing to his colleagues. And eventually he grew to know more African Americans and saw there wasn't such a big difference at all. But in our discussions, it soon became painstakingly obvious that Africa was huge, with so many countries, languages, and cultures that to attempt to teach this massive topic in one class was absurd. With my professor's stories, I also realized that despite all the talk about Africa's glorious past, I knew very little about contemporary Africa. If I depended on nightly news and the paper for info, I would never know.

So my newfound task and lifelong responsibility became that if I were going to call myself African American, I needed to be well versed on contemporary Africa. It also included the recognition that new Africans call America home, too, which for some strange reason never came up when discussing African American life.

IGNORANCE FACTOR

A few years back, I was charged with writing a story on misogyny in hip-hop. *Tip Drill*, a much-maligned song by rapper Nelly, was the controversy of the day in part because in the after-hours music video the St. Louis native swiped a credit card down a black woman's rear. I trekked the halls of college campuses for some quotes from hip-hop fans. Two young African American women agreed to be interviewed. As they went fishing for words to defend their support of sexism and right to love the song, one woman in frustration began pontificating on Africa.

"Wearing no clothes is a part of our culture," she lamented. "People in Africa don't wear clothes." It was a truly WTF moment. I paused, then assessed that this young woman with bright eyes and aptitude was dead serious. "People in Africa wear clothes," I said as calmly as I could. Clouding her embarrassment with extra attitude, she retorted, "Well, how was I supposed to know that?"

The high level of ignorance surrounding Africa among African Americans in general is disturbing to say the least. I once led an African history workshop for a Saturday tutoring program. In the workshop I asked students to name the African countries they knew. I think they came up with ten as a group, and it became painstakingly evident that the other teachers and coordinators knew even less than that. Some, in fact, were irritated that I knew any of the countries at all, probably muttering "show off" when I left the room.

There are plenty of hardworking community groups and universities that seek to reeducate the public; the bulk of the work however, is trapped in academia, trickling down to the masses much like those ineffective trickle-down economics theories. Although the past few decades have been riddled with reaffirmations of blackness in music and cultural activities, these actions are usually void of the concrete realities of Africans or African culture today. Blame it on the American attitude of Americans first, everyone else later, but the prism through which most African Americans view blacks globally is a purely native-born African American one.

Ugochi Nwaogwugwu, the daughter of Nigerian parents of Igbe heritage, is happy for those African Americans who participate in African cultural activities and stay abreast of issues in Africa. It's a start, she says, but it's not nearly enough. "As African Americans, we are very prosperous; it doesn't take anything for us to take a DNA test," she says, referring to the tests popularized in Henry Louis Gates's heritage documentary. In the doc, Gates traced the lineage of African American celebrities including Chris Rock, Maya Angelou, and Tina Turner. "We have the top-notch cars, the clothes, we have whatever we want. All we need is the desire. Even those rich celebrities never thought they could find out where they are from specifically. Africa is the biggest continent in the world, so to say you're African American isn't enough."

NEW AFRICAN IDENTITY

The wave of new African immigrants is transforming the African American identity. No longer can people assume that all blacks have a shared past with slavery, homegrown ties to the South, or an affinity for soul food. As part of the African diaspora there's a shared challenge to colonial powers and racism, but cultural nuances prevail.

While the Caribbean immigrant influence on African American culture is some generations in the making, most of the African immigrant experience was birthed in the involuntary slavery experience. It wasn't until the 1960s, when many African nations achieved independence, that a steady stream of new African immigrants came stateside. Until then, many Africans headed for the European nations that had colonized their homes. Most hailed from the talented, middle-class ranks of English-speaking African nations and were sent to the States for college with the noble intent of returning home to rebuild their countries. Playwright Lorraine Hansberry captured this phenomenon in the play *Raisin in the Sun*, in which Beneatha Younger, a first-generation African American college student, falls head-over-heels in love with Joseph Asagai, a young Yoruban student with dreams of returning to Nigeria as a physician.

But the shift from independence to single-party rule forced many educated Africans who fell out of favor with the ruling parties to find work elsewhere. As government conflicts grew, a growing number of educated Africans found themselves without jobs while others were forced to flee their homelands in fear of political retribution.

A friend of mine, a son of a Liberian statesman, often told stories of how his dad, a high-ranking official, had to flee for his life with the 1980 leadership coup. When his father came to the United States he could find only day-labor jobs while aspiring to a college professorship. "It's like if a Kennedy was run from his home and landed in Malaysia as a box boy," he said.

But this story rang true for many.

The African immigrant population has tripled in the past two decades. Communities of Nigerians, Ghanaians, Ethiopians, Eritrians, Senegalese, Egyptians, Somalians, and South Africans are taking root in urban enclaves and suburbs. By 2000, foreign-born blacks constituted 30 percent of the black population in New York City, 28 percent of the black population in Boston, and about a quarter in Montgomery County, Maryland, an analysis of census data conducted at Queens College shows.

Africans are the most educated immigrant group in the United States, with some 50 percent holding bachelor's degrees. According to the 2000 census, African immigrants are more educated than any other native-born ethnic group, including white Americans, holding twice as many degrees as white Americans and four times as many as native-born African Americans.

"They face more issues of underemployment and not being able to get the kinds of jobs and status that they had at home," said Kelley Johnson, research associate for the United African Organization, an advocacy group for African national organizations. "So you have the doctor who's driving a cab situation."

The 1986 Immigration Reform and Control Act made it easier for undocumented immigrants in the United States to become permanent residents. In 1990, the Diversity Visa Program was introduced as part of the 1990 Immigration Act. The program was designed to promote immigration from underrepresented countries and allow up to fifty thousand Africans annually to come to the United States via a lottery process. A larger number of new immigrants hailed from the former French, Portuguese, and Spanish colonies. With the European immigration pendulum swinging to the right and stricter immigration policies rising, the United States became more attractive to Africans.

"Africans who come to America come to work so they can send money home," said Ugochi Nwaogwugwu, whose parents fled Nigeria during political upheavals in the 1970s. "When they get here, they work and then find they can't go home. Others go abroad and get educated, but there are no opportunities at home so they have to stay abroad. It's almost like you're a prisoner of your new foreign land."

But there's also a blossoming refugee community, says Johnson. In the 2000s, a wave of Tanzanians, Somalians, and Burundians from resettlement camps came to the United States. In many cases, these refugee communities include many artists and artisans with very little education or exposure to Western life.

"[Refugees] often come with a negative view of the black community that they get from Western media," said Johnson. "A lot of the refugee support areas are in mostly white settings. So when they come in they don't have a lot of contact with the African American community. One of the challenges is that people come and identify with their national background and don't think of themselves primarily as black. African Americans think [the refugees] are trying to distance themselves."

In some cases the specific ethnic identity is so strong that there's not a strong sense of *African* identity, a banner, Johnson says, her organization hopes to get the incredibly diverse population of immigrants to embrace to give themselves more leverage in the States.

However, there's a new, very continental wave of African students coming stateside as well as a burgeoning class of second-generation, American-born Africans who bridge cultures seamlessly.

"I had a very wide perspective on life being born here to Ghanaian parents in Chicago," said Yau Agyeman, a young soul singer. His parents came to the United States in the mid-1970s and immediately joined the local Ghanian community. "My parents are Ashanti, and my father for a large portion of time was the treasurer for the Asanteman Association of Chicago," he adds. "Everybody in the culture is your family. My father's friends are my uncles. All of them and I refer to them as Uncle whoever. All of my mom's friends are my aunts. It's a big thing of respect. It's very much the village principle, everyone is hands-on, working together." Agyeman grew up attending Ghanian festivals and celebrations. Except for occasionally being asked ignorant questions, he didn't see the big deal in bridging cultures, a trait Johnson echoes is common in second-generation African immigrants.

"I love being the color that I am, and I love that I have immediate roots in Africa, but in the huge scale of it all, I'm a human being trying to survive."

A RIVER RUNS THROUGH IT

Madieye Gueye, a young, ambitious Senegalese student, couldn't find work in his homeland. It was the mid-1980s, and although Gueye, a Wolof, had a master's degree in economics, he wasn't in favor with the new ruling party in Senegal and knew he'd have to leave the country to survive. He'd met an African American woman in Dakar named Linda, who was on a quest to uncover her roots. "She was very sweet, caring, and generous," says Gueye. "When I was looking at her, I thought I was looking at America."

Gueye came to the United States in 1987 with high hopes that were quickly dashed. "As soon as I got to New York I was cursed; I'd never been cursed in my life." Gueye assumed he would become part of the African American culture at large, but he found that his affinity was often one-sided. "You identify yourself as black; you see a black man like you, you look at him as your brother. But everyone doesn't see it that way."

As Gueye adjusted to American life, he quickly had to accept that most Americans, particularly African Americans, knew next to nothing about Africa, with images of Tarzan, starvation, or wildlife safaris dancing in their heads. "Sometimes I'll have people say, 'Where do you live? Do you live in a tree?'"

But Gueye has learned not to judge and points to schools that simply don't teach the truth.

"Many African Americans don't know what Africa is. You don't want to judge them. Or their schools don't give them the real truth."

Gueye eventually settled in Chicago, where he and his wife, Awa, bustling with entrepreneurial spirit, opened Yassa, the city's first Senegalese restaurant. Although most of the African dining establishments nestled in trendier, mostly white areas on the city's North Side, Gueye opened his on Seventy-Ninth and Cottage Grove, an all-black, working-class area on the South Side.

"People told me it would never work," he says. "But I refused to believe that African American people wouldn't support an African restaurant." Business was slow, and the restaurant struggled for months. But after a few high-profile reviews, the restaurant flooded with customers: mostly white diners from the suburbs at first, but later a multiracial clientele ensued. "People said my restaurant looked like the United Nations," he joked. Within months, the African American clientele soared, but Gueye still struggles to attract patrons from the neighborhood.

"African Americans aren't very adventurous when it comes to food," he laughs. Yet his business's success is a testament to the growing bridge between African immigrants and the community. "I made the right decision and I came to the right place. I see change, I see progress."

CULTURE CLASH

In the 1990s the natural and synthetic braid craze took hold in urban communities. African American women were looking for new styling alternatives that didn't require chemical relaxers or the dreaded scorch of the press and comb. Hair braiding, a tradition that survived the transatlantic slave trade, took on a new life. Many recently arrived African women immigrants with rich hair-braiding traditions and schooling made a killing. Shops popped up everywhere, with some women making four hundred to five hundred dollars per head for their unique services. With scores of women opting for African braiders, traditional salon competitors took notice. The immigrants' shops posed a threat to American-born braiders, too.

The *Chicago Reader* printed an intriguing story by Tasneem Paghdiwala pointing to the fierce competition between African- and American-born black braiders. "I didn't appreciate the signs that I saw Senegalese braiders hanging on their shops when they started coming over here—AUTHENTIC AFRICAN HAIR BRAIDING," said Taalib-Din Uqdah, an American-born celebrity braider in Washington, D.C. "As if what we'd been doing was fake."

Uqdah, head of the American Hairbraiders and Natural Haircare Association, led a coast-to-coast battle to fight against laws that required hair braiders to go to beauty school. He launched the group in 1995 and compared his forays to going toe-to-toe with Jim Crow laws in the beauty industry. Dozens of Chicago-based African braiders were hit with cease-and-desist letters because they hadn't attended beauty school. The African Braiders formed an advocacy group of braiders (African American braiders in the story claimed they were unfamiliar with the group) that later disbanded, and Uqdah was asked to continue their efforts. He tapped Amazon Smiley, an African American braider and mother of the industry in the city. Smiley had opened her business in the city in the late 1970s, trained hundreds, and launched an international braiders association with a thousand members at its peak, but it consisted largely of native-born black braiders, in part, said Smiley, to show that native-born blacks were capable braiders, too. Other American-born stylists in the story complained that African braiders wouldn't share their hair suppliers or trade tips. The African stylists featured claimed that American-born braiders simply didn't know how to braid.

■ ■ ■

Mounting stereotypes on both sides of the black cultural fence foster a staggering friction, with Africans charging that African Americans aren't taking advantage of opportunities and know nothing about Africa and African Americans piping that Africans are arrogant and stay to themselves.

Nwaogwugwu was born in the United States and raised practicing Igbo traditions, but the conflicts she experienced in juggling both cultures led her to write a book on the subject. "People ask me all the time, 'Why do Africans hate us?' I feel like I'm in the middle of this global discussion. I'm African and I'm African American. I've had encounters with Africans who have been really rude to me because they thought I was American. Then I've had African Americans dog Africans out and I had to stop them because they didn't know I was African. I've had Africans come up to me and say I'm not African because I don't have an accent and I wasn't born in the country."

Growing up, Nwaogwugwu felt a constant tug and pull in balancing both African and African American traditions. "It's always a challenge bridging the two," she says, pointing to differences in dating, reverence to elders, and family structure. "In Africa, the kids don't have a voice," she says. "Parents in Africa dictate what your life will be like; in America that's a big call for rebellion."

But the conflicts go beyond cultural nuances, with both entitlement and authentic blackness being questioned.

No one disputes that both native-born and immigrant African Americans face discrimination. Amadou Diallo's murder by New York City police was a reminder of color's role in police brutality. However, there have been some recent debates regarding affirmative action in universities. Harvard University, in recognizing that over two-thirds of their African American students are immigrants, wondered if they were underserving the descendants of slaves, whom affirmative action was initially created for.

In other cases, the "who's really black and who's not" debate pops up. While running against Barack Obama for the Illinois Senate, Alan Keyes, a perennial right-wing political figure, charged that he had a more "authentic" African American experience than Obama because his ancestors overcame slavery. On the other hand, an island-born immigrant and editor I worked with when writing on Obama's senatorial bid asked me to emphasize Obama's immigrant status.

"Ask him if he thinks being the son of an immigrant gave him a determination that traditional African Americans don't have," he said.

"Why would I ask that?"

"Because," he replied, "you-all just don't have the drive of the immigrant," which I found ironic considering he worked for a publication owned by descendants of slaves. Nevertheless, I followed his guidelines reluctantly, and Obama, who surely must have heard this issue before, responded that he didn't see any difference between the black immigrants who crossed waters to be here or the blacks who left rural areas in the South and came north during the Great Migration. Both were looking for better lives for themselves and their families, he said. Both had overcome tremendous obstacles in doing so.

Sanity at last.

3

BRIDGES
BIRACIAL, BICULTURAL IDENTITY

*Biracial and bicultural
Americans embrace
their role in the African
American experience.*

Ebony magazine asked me to write a story on blacks who were often mistaken for being white. Initially, I didn't think I'd find much. The 1950s flicks *Pinkie* and *Imitation of Life* had explored the "looking white" or "tragic mulatto syndrome," and I figured in this post–"black is beautiful," post–civil rights movement era, neither blacks nor whites cared much about it. But I was shocked by the horror stories of very light-skinned blacks who hopped between defending blacks among whites who thought they were white and claiming blackness among blacks who thought *they* thought they were better because they looked white. Most of the people interviewed were African Americans with no biracial heritage but with a significant dose of miscegenation in their lineage that showed up in their appearance. Raised in African American worlds, they resented this look and felt that any advantages blacks assumed they received were nothing more than a double-edged sword. At least one person interviewed resented that people assumed she was biracial. "I had a black mother and a black father. I know who I am, and I know how to comb my hair," she asserted.

I was referred to Keri Lowder, a green-eyed, blond-haired woman with an African American mother and Norwegian father and the only biracial woman interviewed. "I tell people that I'm African American and that I have a white father," Lowder says, noting she would never tell people she is white. As for the biracial label, she said, "My sister looks like Halle Berry so they know that she's half black. So if she says she's biracial, she's not denying her blackness. If I say I'm black, I'm not denying my white heritage because it's there staring right at you."

She told me a story about her NCAA track championships in Boise, Idaho. Each time she stepped onto the floor the crowd would erupt in thunderous applause. "It was very strange, because they weren't clapping for anyone else," she said. It didn't make much sense until she fell, injured, and found herself alone with a white trainer who let racial epitaphs demeaning the all-black track teams flow from her lips like water. "She thought I was white," Lowder recalled. As for the crowd's cheers, "They thought I was some great white hope," said Lowder, who proclaimed she was in fact black and in so many words told the trainer how she felt. However, the thirtysomething mom recalls being pulled over by white cops because she was riding shotgun with her black boyfriends. And the reactions she gets from white Americans who discover that her mother is black range from intense anger to firecracker curiosity. "I become the great interpreter," said Lowder.

BLACK GIRL TURNED EXOTIC

Growing up, I didn't know biracial identity was such a social trigger. Most biracial kids I grew up with in my mostly black, family-friendly neighborhood on the South Side were black as far as the other kids were concerned, and in most cases as far as they were concerned, too. My childhood best friend's mother was Scottish, a point she clarified whenever we accidentally referred to her mom as English. At all of ten years old, my friend was crystal clear on her identity. "If you have one drop of black blood, you're black," she said firmly. Not that we questioned it, but in case we wanted to, the line was drawn in the sand.

That was pretty much my take on the matter; anybody with any African ancestry was black. I couldn't get too picky about the matter because my own lineage, like most African Americans, consisted of a blend of cultural influences, so if I ever dreamed of calling out a kid for having a white parent, I could very well lift up my own rug of racial intermingling, too.

While applying for admission to an all-black academic center, someone suggested to my mom that I could pass as biracial and marked "white" on the racial identity question to give me an edge in a school that needed to integrate in reverse. My mother refused. "I just didn't think it would be fair to your father to say he's white," my mom, a lighter-skinned woman herself, said. I don't think it crossed her mind that the woman in question was suggesting that she, not my brown-skinned father, could be the one who passed.

Nevertheless, it wasn't until junior high that I stumbled upon the "declare yourself" mentality. A green-eyed girl with light brown hair and caramel skin whose name I can no longer remember found herself in a crossfire of torpedoed whispers. The black students thought she was black, the white students thought she was white. I don't think anyone actually asked her, so they hung on baited breath, hoping she'd drop hints. Little by little, we learned that her parents were white and that she lived on the South Side in a multiracial neighborhood. One day, surely feeling the bubbling whispers rattling the school floorboard, she out and said she was white, a revelation that didn't satisfy anyone and certainly wasn't consistent with the racial determinants we'd been raised with. She was simply too dark to be white. The black kids figured she just didn't know. "Maybe she's adopted," they concluded.

But the pedal hit the metal when, in college, the term "exotic" started floating around. Marking an end to the "Nubian sisters" tributes and African heritage shout-outs, the new typhoon of hip-hop and R & B videos redecorated the beauty landscape in the late 1990s with a parade of mostly fair-skinned black and biracial beauties. The question du jour became "What are you?" One rapper talked of wanting a woman with "Chinese eyes, Indian hair, and a black-girl ass." Shout-outs were given to women who were "Spanish and black," "Polish and black," and "Asian and black," and the pop culture fever tapped a nerve, implying that to be simply a black beauty was not enough.

Between the exotic fever and Atlanta's colorism history, I found myself at the heart of an unlikely crossfire, too, with "What are you?" hurled at me several times weekly. At first I thought it was a joke, but the questions and comments kept coming. When I heard "You're too pretty to be black" uttered from one college boy's lips, I was a half a second from forging his beat down. At least one guy asked me out and was disheartened to learn that I wasn't Latina. Another guy, in a typical tirade about imperialism and racism, apologized for offending me and my white ancestors. A nine-year-old white boy pointed to me and yelled to his parents, "Look, Ma, a mixed girl!" and they rushed him off before I could respond. The ridiculousness was dizzying. But others—strangers, mind you— wanted to wage full-scale arguments, fire rising to their temples as they tried to out-debate me on myself.

"What are you?" a slim guy eager to get my number asked.

"Black."

"Black and what else?"

"Just black."

"And what else?"

"Nothing."

"I think you're black, Chinese, and Indian," he said.

I don't give a flying fig what you think is what I wanted to say, wanting to walk away but not willing to risk being called out by name and possibly responding inappropriately.

"Like I said, I'm black."

"Why are you being like that?" he asked.

"Like what?" I asked.

"I'm asking a question, and you're acting like you're too good to answer."

"I answered your question," I said.

"What are you trying to prove?" he asked, then he walked off, highly pissed and ranting to his ragtag boys about me lying and telling him I was black.

And these were all conversations with black people. But after shouting that I was black a thousand times over, I started to wonder why I didn't feel the need to explain. Why did the inference of biracial or multiracial identity irritate me so?

First off, randomly asking "What are you?" has got to be one of the most ignorant questions on the planet, and yet perfect strangers at bus stops feel they have a constitutional right to know. I didn't think it was anyone's business. Most of the interracial mixing, at least in my family line, wasn't this voluntary, love-based experience but a direct result of miscegenation typical in the slavery and postslavery periods. This doesn't lend itself to pride in being, say, part Irish or English. While both my mother's and father's sides claim some Native American ancestry, we don't know names or tribes, and any cultural nuances passed through the generations have been lost. So while I'm in touch with native history, culturally, it would be an insult to Native Americans for me to say I'm native, too. But most black people with pre–Civil War roots in the western hemisphere have some mix of these cultures, so what makes mine any different from anyone else's?

Furthermore, I, like Lowder, felt I'd be denying my black pride if I so much as mentioned other influences, as if to give credence to them implied I thought I was "better than." And the "better than" history of colorism, with black elitism equating lighter skin with higher status and beauty, had wedged a great enough divide that anyone with any black consciousness didn't want to be confused as "better than" because of color or phenotype. The pain was so deep that to embrace any non-African lineage with affection by default minimized the African experience in America and was perceived as disrespect to your ancestors and our nation's polarized past. I didn't want to be one of those color-struck types whose multicultural past was wielded like a badge of one-upmanship and a passport to escapism.

At first I thought people inquired because the status of "other" was more intriguing than black—another dose of internalized racism people had bought into. In other cases, I figured people used it to justify diversity in lifestyles, interests, and mannerisms that didn't fit neatly into the African American box. If you're black and, say, read books on belly dancing or have some international flair about you, you must be something other than African American. I was at a flamenco show once where my teacher performed, and I was grilled by a young white patron who didn't understand why I was there. She insisted that I must be an intern. But when my African American date wowed the table by having a full conversation with a Japanese immigrant in her native tongue, instantly the young white patrons wanted to know where we were from, because we couldn't possibly be just regular black people from the United States.

After the ten thousandth "What are you?" I decided to ease up on the defensiveness and figured people just don't know. Nor would it kill me if I responded that I had native and white ancestry, since we talked about it freely at family reunions all the time. Besides, I wondered, would my native ancestors feel I was denying them if I said I was African American and didn't so much as mention them? I don't know. But for the record, when the next census comes around, I'm marking "black."

My brother gets a lot of questions about whether he's part Asian. My brown-skinned sister is often mistaken for being from southern India. "I have a lot of people asking if I am Laotian," she said. "I don't get it." But Nate Quinn, a painter friend of mine in New York City, had a similar experience. "Growing up, nobody thought I was anything but black," said Quinn, a fair-skinned guy with soft curls. "Now, people ask me what I am daily. Am I Dominican, Cuban, from Ecuador? Am I biracial? I'm thinking, 'What the hell is going on?'"

Because I'm not biracial but often mistaken for it, I understand the frustrations over the flippish questions. I understand the fierce claim to blackness sometimes over other heritages, in response to the "other" divide. At the same time, it makes nothing but sense for a person raised in two cultures to embrace and take pride in both, and yet I get why some black people just want them to claim black.

COLORISMS

Lailana Hickerson doesn't get why everyone wants to call Barack Obama the first black president. "He's biracial," she says. "Why can't they just call him the first biracial president?" Hickerson, an artist in her twenties whose mother is Filipina and father is African American, explores biracial identity in her comic book *My Hafu*, the story of a black and Japanese teen coming of age. "The first thing people ask is 'What is she? Is she Hawaiian?'" said Hickerson, who gets more questions about race than technique. "Not a lot of multiracial children are portrayed in the media."

Hickerson's father met her mom while stationed in the Philippines, and she was raised in both black and multiracial neighborhoods in New Jersey.

"My parents made it a strong point to be conscious of who you are as a person first," said Hickerson, who was raised largely by her mother and later sought out opportunities to reconnect with black culture. "My father said you are 100 percent of myself and 100 percent of your mother." But friends and strangers often pressured her to choose. "They'd say the black gene is stronger, when people look at you, your skin color is brown, so you're automatically black. I can't accept one world without accepting the other."

Once, while speaking at a conference for black artists, Hickerson was asked to discuss her art and biracial identity. "People would come up to me afterward and say, 'You are African American, you know that, right?' I'd say, 'I'm also Filipino American,' but they took offense."

She compares the pressure to choose with people just wanting you to be on their team. "I guess people just want to know that you identify with them, too."

But Hickerson doesn't get why African Americans, biracial or otherwise, don't embrace their varied backgrounds. "I find it very interesting that you have people who classify themselves as being black and they're of lighter skin, but it's clear that they have multiracial identity. Or you talk to a guy whose mother is white, and he denies her by saying he's black. Maybe it's just easier to pick one."

BALANCING ACT

A military brat, Gregory Johnson split his childhood between small towns in Spain and Tampa, Florida. His father met his mother in Aragon, Spain, where Johnson was born in the mid-1970s. His father came from a family steeped in African American pride and traditions: educators, HBCU grads, NAACP activists, and Bahamian missionaries, and his mom hailed from a proud family that rebelled against fascism. "I'm just proud that I come from two hardworking families with very strong traditions," says Johnson.

When his parents divorced, his mother married another African American man in the military, and Johnson spent time on military bases in Italy and later Madrid, where he was one of many biracial children. Johnson, a history buff, finds deep parallels between Spain's fight against fascism and civil rights struggles for blacks in the States, yet he also recognizes the ironies, pointing to the history of the black Moors in Spain, the racial symbolism of the bullfight, and a stuffed African man in a Spanish museum. "You talk about double identity, it's weird to be on those two sides of the colonized and the colonizer," he said. "I chalk it up to the world and try to be honest with myself."

But his families were very mindful of raising Johnson in healthy environments. He has as many jovial tales of his proud Spanish uncles walking him through the streets of Aragon as he does of the Bahamian folktales his grandmother shared with him as a kid. When it was time to go to college, Johnson followed in the footsteps of his father's family and headed for Morehouse College, a historically black college for men.

"Some people thought I was on that 'light-skinned kid trying to get in touch with his roots' thing, but at an HBCU you're in the African diaspora. Some of everybody's there. Are you going to be the new kid who doesn't adjust or are you going to break those walls and fit in?"

While Johnson is well aware of the criticism black men get for dating white women, he never internalized angst against his parents. "I get those e-mails, the 'look which black men have white women' messages. But where do we draw the line if they're making solid contributions?" he asks, noting that both A. Phillip Randolph, union pioneer, and music legend Quincy Jones married white women and yet made advancements for blacks.

Is he, I asked, a Spanish man? "Funny you ask," he replied, and told a story of his grandmother showing him off in beaming maternal mode to friends on the street. A friendly old woman shook her finger in his face, telling him never to forget that he's a Spaniard and to know what that means. He paused during our interview, and then referenced W. E. B. Dubois's double consciousness theory, which explores the conflicts of being both black and American. "You have to declare blackness; it's a fact of being in this country."

However, he notes that Latin American cultures are a good model for balancing his hybrid mix of racial identity. Cubans, Dominicans, and Brazilians have been able to find harmony among African, Spanish, Portuguese, and Native American cultures and religions, he points out. "I can relate to Latino culture," he says. Now that he has a young daughter with a Haitian mother, he's wondering how to incorporate her diverse lineage into her childhood experience.

RECLAIMING A CULTURE

I read once that Harlem-reared pop star Kelis didn't know her mother, a half-Asian, half–Puerto Rican woman, wasn't black until Kelis was nearly in high school.

So when my friend Chris Chaney told me he didn't know he was half Puerto Rican until he was nearly a junior in high school, I wasn't surprised. "I just thought my mother was a light-skinned black woman," Chaney said. "Actually, my African American father is lighter than my mother." With American racism forcing browner Latinos to choose, Chaney said, his Puerto Rican grandparents raised their kids in New York City largely as black Americans. "Both my grandparents were from Puerto Rico and raised their children to speak English, and they wanted them to assimilate."

"Because of their complexion, they initially had trouble with other Puerto Ricans because they looked like black kids and didn't know how to speak the language," adds Chaney. Most of his cultural exposure came from his grandparents, he says, noting the music, the dancing, and the food. "We roast a pig on the Fourth of July, we have paella on Christmas." But the experience was absent of the language. "I think you get that with a lot of dark Hispanics."

While Chaney says that technically he's biracial, his browner skin and African features don't scream multicultural. Raised in New York City's projects, Chaney grew up immersed in a mostly African American culture. "I could clearly exist as a black person and no one would be the wiser. But it's really my own personal pride that makes me mention it and embrace it. And my affinity for my grandparents."

In college and later as an adult, Chaney made strides to study the culture: he took Puerto Rican history and Spanish classes, went to the Puerto Rican parade, and canvassed Spanish museums. He even advocated for a Latino issue of the magazine he works for. But his knowledge of Spanish is minimal, a barrier that keeps him from totally immersing himself in the culture. "If I spoke Spanish, I could exist in two worlds," he said. "But without the language, I'm an African American man with Puerto Rican lineage."

Chaney does remember being a kid and bragging to his black friends that he was half Puerto Rican, which they totally dismissed. "I thought it made me better than them in that I had something they didn't have. Like having cable and they didn't," he says, laughing.

Embracing the culture just helps in this very transcultural world, he says, and he wonders if his limited Spanish hurts his professional opportunities. "I tease my mother and say you could have really helped me out if you taught me Spanish. She said she didn't know enough of it. Besides, it's just fun to be immersed in another culture."

BLACK, WHITE, OR OTHER

The 2000 census campaign launched massive efforts to count African Americans. Its census takers loaded up with T-shirts, buttons, and key rings, the Bureau hoped to encourage African Americans who traditionally avoided the census to stand up and be counted. Census stats were used to allocate government dollars, and the more African Americans included, the more money would be assigned to address black issues and communities. But the 2000 census also marked the beginning of another campaign. Hoping to address the burgeoning biracial community, the category of "other" was introduced. While biracial activists praised this addition because they would no longer be forced to choose, some African American activists mounted a counter-campaign asking biracial Americans to mark "black." I remember debating the issue with a friend of mine who worked for the census. Why, I wondered, couldn't they just mark both? "If every biracial person marks 'other,' black communities lose money. Besides, most black people are multiracial, and you don't see us checking off all these boxes. It's silly," she said, and then she reiterated the one-drop rule.

Every biracial person has faced the racial map box. Torn between splitting identities, forced to choose one over the other, feels akin to ranking your mom over your dad.

Keri Lowder was confronted with "the choice" in kindergarten, when a test asked her to identify her race. "I didn't know whether to pick black or white," said Lowder, who was raised to say she was both. So she asked the teacher, who asked the principal, who told her to mark "black."

Lailana Hickerson said she switched up from year to year, marking "black" one year and "Asian" the next. Now she marks "other."

When Gregory Johnson returned to Florida as a teen after a stint in Spain, he was faced with new Tampa busing regulations. If he marked anything but "black," he made the quota to go to his neighborhood school. If he marked "black," he'd be bused across town. "My mother was like, 'What's the big deal? Just mark whatever will allow you to go to the school down the street.' I wanted to go to school down the street. But I had to make a racial statement. I was reading Malcolm X and reading my grandmother's *Black World*. So I went to school forty-five minutes away by bus."

Even Chris Chaney, who identifies himself as African American when faced with the option, will pick "other" if he can't mark both.

"Did you know that there's a controversy about 'other'? Some people say it takes away government-allotted funding from programs for blacks," I mentioned to him.

"Really?"

"Yep. It's like you're taking money away from the black community if you mark both."

"You gotta be kidding," he said. It was all ironic because most of Chaney's work is dedicated to improving business and community relations for African Americans.

"Nope." Suddenly, with one mark of the X, all his hard work and volunteering would go down the whitewashing drain.

"I can understand that," he said. "But what am I supposed to do? I can't deny my grandparents."

And once again, this debate between defending intra-ethnic identity and fighting against the powers of institutionalized racism seemed wildly out of place and against our better wisdom, and we laughed.

4

BLACK, GAY, LESBIAN, AND PROUD

GLBT IN BLACK AMERICA

K-OSS is a comic book character who wrestles with his sexual identity.

I went to a swank club on Chicago's North Side to meet a colleague of mine—an openly gay television producer in town with a few of his friends by way of New York. He was looking for a fun night in the city between grueling workdays, and someone recommended that he come here. Friends in tow, he, along with the other mid-week, mostly black partyers, downed martinis between rounds on the dance floor.

The night was easy. But all that stopped when the nightclub's eager promoter yanked the music to usher on the talent of the night—a comedian. The crowd, anxious to mingle, was largely disinterested but gave him their well-mannered attention anyway, hoping polite indifference would rush the act along.

The comedian, sensing the crowd's pending disengagement, be-gan digging in his bag of save-me tricks. He pulled out the tried-and-true: a gay joke. He poked fun at the way gay black men dance, playing a portion of a house music cut and vogueing à la 1990s Madonna and swaying in the clichéd way of comedians desperate to imitate.

But no one laughed.

If he had told this joke maybe ten to fifteen years before Ellen Degeneres came out, before *Six Feet Under* or M'chelle Ndegocello or the legalization of gay partnerships, maybe his joke would have coaxed a sympathetic ear. But we were a few years shy of 2010, a new world in which "gay" no longer meant "other" but applied to our family, friends, coworkers, and favorite celebs. Gayness for the sake of gayness just wasn't funny. The eager-to-please comic's sen-sibility was a full 180 degrees off. The homosexual tolerance meter had shifted, and the comic stood frozen and, I'm sure, stunned by the changing times.

His mistakes were fatal: (1) He assumed that an all-black au-dience was innately homophobic. That we're so hypermasculine that anything gay is fundamentally funny. While this is a common depiction of us in the mainstream, this blanket stereotype is too broad. (2) He assumed (and you know what those assumptions make you) that the all-black audience was uniformly heterosexual. That you can't be black and gay. If for some reason there are black gays, they would not be in a club like this on anything other than "gay night." (3) He assumed that the all-black audience didn't actually *know* any gay people, or if they did, that their interactions didn't scratch beyond the surface, that they didn't have close or even amicable relationships with gay people. But this comic wasn't talking about some Martian group we'd all observed from afar, but rather someone's brother, friend, colleague, or someone in the audience themselves. (4) It never dawned on the poor comedian that a producer could be in the audience, one who might want to scoop up new talent. And apparently, it never occurred to this comic that that producer would be gay.

The joke fell like a bed of rocks, and the promoter swiftly put the music back on. My friend and his friends knocked out a few more drinks and returned to the dance floor.

■ ■ ■

Homosexuality never came up for discussion when I was growing up. It wasn't part of the nightly dinner-table conversations, and it didn't fit neatly into those requisite birds-and-the-bees sit-downs either. Oddly enough, it didn't even come up in sex education. On the playground, kids hurled unflattering terms at other kids who seemed to exhibit some traditional characteristics of the sex they weren't. But you were neither for homosexuality nor against it, because it wasn't even on the table for an opinion.

All that stopped when I arrived in Atlanta in the mid-1990s with the other fresh-faced college kids aiming to take the world by storm. We were overwhelmed by a gay culture openly rooted in the black community—a population we had been told didn't exist. Students open to a new understanding of the sexual spectrum were hit on by both sexes, much to our confusion and amusement, and many had to rethink their outlook on the sexes completely.

Atlanta's blossoming gay and lesbian black population was a safe haven for those wrestling with their sexual orientation, playing much the role San Francisco does for white gay men. Friends began to "come out." And the stories of growing numbers of associates who claimed a different take on sexuality mounted with each semester's end. At one point, it seemed as if everyone could be or was gay. Suddenly, what was once never discussed was always discussed, and the coming-out revelations stockpiled to the point of normalcy.

So by the time I graduated from college, to learn that a friend was now gay, bi, or lesbian was not even as intriguing as discovering they'd moved to Canada, dyed their hair, or landed a hot gig in Silicon Valley. A year or so after college, Ethan, a college buddy who worked with me on a few TV productions, called to tell me the obvious.

"I'm gay," he revealed.

"Congratulations, Ethan, but I knew that already."

"That's what everyone keeps saying. You guys are so supportive."

DON'T ASK, DON'T TELL . . . WHO IS, WHO ISN'T

The black community has a very curious relationship with GLBT African Americans.

One response is the "don't ask, don't tell" philosophy—a communal gag order by which people bind and duct-tape their mouths and cover their eyes when the subject surfaces. In many circles the subject is simply not discussed, or not discussed above a whisper. While some who adopt this mode are homophobic, others feel it's simply TMI—too much information. So collectively, in the name of social protocol, politeness, and peace, the topic is avoided in the black community.

I think about the story of a cousin in his forties, the stepfather of two and father of one, who made the long-distance coming-out phone call to his great-aunt down south.

"Auntie, I'm gay," he said.

"We're all gay for the Lord," she said.

"No, really, I'm gay," he chimed.

"And we're all gay when we pray, baby."

After a few more confusing exchanges, the guy gave up and said his good-byes.

When retelling the story, his aunt said, "Oh, I knew exactly what he was saying, but I wasn't going to let him tell me that way."

In other words, she couldn't have cared less. And her cloaked denial was her way of saying *I love you but don't expect me to engage in conversations on the matter.* In fact, he could sit at her breakfast table with his new lover if he liked, but if he brought up the notion of his sexuality, that breakfast plate would be snatched up before he could blink.

The other approach is so diametrically opposed to the first that it's near impossible to believe that they sprout from the same culture. It's what I call the full-blast mode—something akin to a ride on Front Street, with homosexuality the hot matter on the tip of the gossipers' wagging tongues, accusing everyone from their favorite R & B star to the handsome unwed guy of being gay. E-mails detailing which stars are gay and which aren't fly over the Internet like a cyberspace forest fire. And the oohs and aahs related to the "who is and who isn't" question are riddled with paranoia. While at least this approach requires extensive conversation on the matter, it's so salacious that fact merges with fiction, and any real talk about day-to-day gay life is equivalent to a yawn. The witch hunt is sexier. According to this logic, pretty much anything that isn't run-of-the-mill middle-America lifestyle could deem you gay. If you're a man who gets regular manicures and facials, you could be gay.

The result? *Are you gay?* and *Are you a lesbian?* and *Are you bi?* outchart *What's your sign?* as the most frequent questions swirling around the black dating circuit.

DL REVEALED

Robert Walker's comic book *Cyberdelete* pushes all the conventional buttons. The story centers around an African American, Harlem-born soldier in a special military unit and an übersexy techie genius who doubles as a superhero, aka Delete. She's flanked by a crew of multiracial issue-battling hero friends, including a circle of HIV-positive heroes on a mission to destroy the virus. Walker pulls out all the stops. One character in the story is named K-OSS. He's a DL brother terrified that his sexual orientation will be revealed.

"I just feel it's a really big issue in our community," Walker said. "I hope that people who identify with K-OSS will feel free to come out."

Nothing drives a conversation on gay subject matters in the African American community more than the down low, or DL, fire-bomb. "DL" is the term for men in relationships with women who have secret liaisons with other men. While this lifestyle isn't new in any community, it snowballed into the hot topic of the decade and lit a fire to the full-blast-mode approach to gay issues. The mainstreaming all began in the mid-1990s with bisexual author E. Lynn Harris and his sexy, fictitious tales of robust men—both athletes and sought-after, suit-and-tie-wearing professionals—who hid their secret love affairs with other men from their wives and girlfriends.

Suddenly, women were giving every guy the side-eye, so to speak, as they tried to uncover just who was DL and who wasn't. The DL curiosity paralleled the stark rise in AIDS rates among African American women, with a staggering number of cases linked to women whose sex partners were men who either were having sex or had had sex with other men.

This was followed by the gay rapper hysteria, a red scare of sorts, that hit the hip-hop community. People tried to uncover the "secret identity" of popular rappers in the closet. Rumors circulated; second- and thirdhand accounts surfaced of people who'd spotted various male rappers sleeping together. Articles on "gay thugs" and analyses of hip-hop imagery as homoerotic became part of the hip-hop literature, and people were talking.

But all of this was like those early years when scientists warned against global warming; there wasn't any hard evidence that people could cling to. No person on record had come out to validate the DL lifestyle, and it hovered like a cloud in Rumorville. But it all peaked when the book *Down Low*, the true story of a married African American man who had relationships with other men, hit the talk circuit. The inconvenient truth of the DL circus is that it gave validity to the storm of rumors, matched a face to a lifestyle, and scared sexually active men and women half to death.

When I was assigned to interview the *Down Low* author, he was speaking to a crowd of mostly heterosexual women all gripped with fear as he rehashed the tales of choice liaisons and hookups in his book. Prior to the forum's kick-off, I spoke to the lone man in the crowd, a fortyish gay African American who sat quietly by himself. He shared with me privately that he felt the gay community was being unfairly attacked because of DL culture. As a man who was very open about his sexuality, he was confused by those who chose to live double lives.

But the most startling revelation from the author forum was not the author's affairs but rather his summation of his identity. Despite his same-sex conquests, he was adamant about declaring that he was not gay. Nor was he bi. He didn't like any of these labels and could not identify with them. He grew up as an African American man strongly rooted in African American traditions, he said, whereby family values and religion were very important, and the gay lifestyle popularized on TV was completely foreign.

It was a logic that took hold among men who slept with men in black communities. The argument went that "gay" was a culture, whereas sex with someone of the same gender was an act. In fact, many health organizations, prompted by the Centers for Disease Control, now use terms like "men who sleep with men" in their HIV research targeting black and Latino men, because not all men who have sex with other men identify themselves as gay. But like most issues in the African American community, what seemed like a microcosm insight was actually a growing trend for the nation at large. Many people moved away from the gay and lesbian labels, a point that frustrated some gay and lesbian activists who felt their fight for respect was being undermined.

Referring to a national trend in which many GLBTs in their twenties aren't identifying their sexuality, one activist asked, "How are we supposed to study the population if they don't want to be labeled?" The question was posed to an audience of several hundred gay, lesbian, and bisexual activists and academics at a 2008 conference on gender, race, and sexuality held in Chicago. "How are we supposed to get funding for GLBT issues if people don't want to be called gay or lesbian?"

If I'd closed my eyes and switched out a word or two, I could have been standing at an NAACP conference, because the topic centered on identity.

OUTSIDE THE BOX

"I had no gay role models growing up," Ethan said.

A thirty-three-year-old Texas-born Atlanta resident who works in advertising, Ethan was raised in an upper-middle-class home by traditional parents who ran a family business he's worked to avoid.

"I didn't know I was gay until I was in high school," Ethan told me. "The only gay person I knew was this friend of one of my dad's first cousins named Jerry. And I didn't want to be like Jerry. The only gay people we knew growing up were Liberace and Rock Hudson, and they both died of AIDS. I didn't want to be like Jerry, and I didn't want to die of AIDS."

A lot has changed since Ethan's childhood years. The conversation about sexual identity has filtered into the black mainstream, with pop culture references and growing news coverage of gay pride, gay marriage bans, and more. The most notable difference may be the growing panoramic view of GLBT lifestyles.

"I don't want to feel like someone is boxing me in and saying this is what gay people do," said Ethan. "There is no cookie-cutter version of what gay is, just like there's no cookie-cutter view of what black is. My last boyfriend was a football-watching, beer-guzzling, gay black guy. They do exist." Other things have stayed the same. "Gay characters are still the punch line. Not that I don't find it funny," he says. But other than his sexual orientation, Ethan feels largely removed from the gay community.

"I don't really participate in activities that I feel are gay-identified," he said. "I can't think of anything I've done recently that was targeted toward a gay audience." He doesn't go to gay clubs, he doesn't belong to any gay organizations or community groups, nor is he a regular at the pride parade. "Most of my friends are straight," he adds.

As for the raging debate on gay marriage: "I can't imagine two men getting married. I wasn't raised that way," he says. "But if they want to be as miserable as these hetero relationships out here, go right ahead."

In fact, Ethan describes gay pride as "anticlimactic."

"I don't feel I have to jump out and shout and say, *I'm proud to be gay*. I'm not ashamed to be gay. I don't think everyone wants to know that. It's not really their business," he said. "It's not my responsibility to educate people on my sexuality. I'm just trying to be me."

BISEXUAL MEDIUMS

I interviewed a woman who headed a support group for African American bisexual women. In the early 2K, female sexuality was the new It bag of fashion and hip-hop, and references to threesomes—women loving women for the pleasure of men—were charted like half notes across the pop culture scene. But the woman I interviewed, a mom in her thirties with a young son, had had previous relationships with both men and women, and she wasn't thrilled with the new media attention. She felt it whittled down her lifestyle choices and dilemmas into a purely sexual circus act.

"I'm not some sex-craved woman," she said. "I'm looking for a meaningful relationship, too."

I once heard actress Rosie O'Donnell describe sexuality as very fluid. While some people are at one of two extremes, being either gay or straight, there is a notable gray area. It's this gray area where traditional categories just don't apply. There are black women with dreams of marrying Mr. Right who have had women lovers, but they hesitate to use the label "bisexual."

"I came out to myself first," said Kelley, a community organizer in her midthirties who works with an organization for gay and bi black women. While a college student in Boston, she initially identified herself as bisexual, although she'd never had a relationship with a guy. But coming out was a nightmare: "My mom found out because she read my journal. Both she and my dad approached me after my sophomore year. There was a bit of denial. There was a lot of head butting. My mom was not receptive to me being gay." While her family stewed in disappointment, her friends at school were largely supportive. But it made going home over the summers even more difficult.

"My girlfriend's family was very open, and mine wasn't," she said. Eventually she wrote her family a letter about the stress she felt at home and began to spend holidays with her girlfriend's family. More than a decade later, she says her relationship with her family has evolved tremendously. "I never thought I could say that my dad, my aunt, my girlfriend, and I went to lunch. My dad's moved from being a silent partner to being very warm. Even though my mom hasn't come around in the same way, she no longer makes the hurtful statements that she used to make in the past. It's really amazing how things can change."

Growing up, Kelley says, she doesn't recall hearing any family discussions about homosexuality, although she did have a distinct feeling that being homosexual and being black were somehow diametrically opposed.

"I do remember certain things said in the past that led me to believe that my mom associated gayness with whiteness and that it was something black people shouldn't participate in. It stemmed from this notion that gayness is a European import and that it's not natural or intrinsic to black people. She'd say, 'White people can be gay, but we as black people can't afford to do that kind of stuff.' But you are what you are."

Kelley's mom's belief is one I've run across before. And it stems from two deeply rooted thought processes. The collective progress of African American people in battling institutional racism depended on the actions of people who were of the highest moral fiber. Her upstanding character was allegedly the reason Rosa Parks, a smart, mild-mannered NAACP secretary, was asked to kick off the Montgomery bus boycott instead of a Southern honor student who had been previously tapped but was quickly dropped when she became pregnant. It was the reason activist-scholar Bayard Rustin, an openly gay adviser to Dr. King during the boycott, was asked to lower his profile. Homosexuality was grouped with other questionable or immoral behaviors, and the cost of its exposure was the progress of black people itself.

The other line of thought comes from a black nationalist strain that reasons that African American people have been so corrupted by American white culture that they've adopted behaviors that are counter to their African heritage, particularly the concept of manhood. Black men have been the main targets in overt racist strategies and tactics for emasculation, ranging from genital mutilation during slavery to getting arrested for driving while black today. Again homosexuality is bottled with absent fatherhood, joblessness, and crime as pathologies cultivated by institutional racism.

However, the delicate relationship between race and sexuality can be mind-boggling, Kelley says. "Not that there's a contradiction between being black and gay. There are times when gay people drive me nuts. I have problems with the way white gay people look at things. Black people being hung and the civil rights struggle for African Americans are not the same as gay people struggling for the right to marry. On the other hand some of the most heinous hate crimes committed have been against transgenders. I often find myself upset with black people who say you can't cite overly simplistic similarities between civil rights for blacks and marriage for gays, and at the same time as a gay person you can't act like our only struggle is our desire to get married. Maybe we as African Americans can take pride in launching the civil rights movement, but civil rights are for everyone."

GAY MARRIAGE

On the same day America elected its first black president, the people of California voted to block gay marriage by supporting the hotly contested Proposition 8. Some 70 percent of African Americans in California supported the bill. The irony of it didn't escape the ranks of bloggers and advocates, some of whom quickly fingered the black community's homophobia for the dissolution of gay marriage rights in the state.

"It was so unfair," said Kelley, who noted that California's black population is very small. "I think the discourse on Prop 8 is very problematic. You would look at this and think black people just pushed this thing through. But a whole lot of white people and people of other races pushed it through. I don't think it's an accident that it came on the heels of a black man coming into office."

I had a very strange debate with a straight, California-reared, black male friend of mine we'll call Rick. A former athlete turned businessman, Rick has no issues with homosexuality. He has gay and bi friends, associates, coworkers, and the like. Frankly, he couldn't care less about a person's sexuality. But he is very big on keeping such matters private, which is why he voted to dissolve gay marriage in his state. I, not residing in California and having no issues with the marriage debate, didn't understand how he could be in favor of gay rights but against gay marriage.

"Why should a gay person have to tell people that they're gay?" he argued. "A lot of gay people want to keep that private. Why should they have to declare themselves through marriage?"

"What if they want to?" I asked.

"They already have legalized partnership."

"That's not the same."

"What's the difference?"

"The ceremony, the concept of acceptance."

"They can have a ceremony."

"But it's not official. It's not the same thing."

"If he's gay, he shouldn't have to declare that. What if he doesn't want his coworkers to know? Do you know the impact marriage could have on his business?"

We argued on and on, but the point remains that there's more to why African Americans voted to support Prop 8, and the reasons don't fit neatly into the "blacks are more traditional and more religious" box. There has been little to no public conversation about how the black community in general can support gay rights but oppose gay marriage and why a sizable number of GLBT African Americans likewise do not support gay marriage. However, the fact that there is a range of opinions on the issue stays muffled and under the radar, much like the subject of choice and sexuality in general.

REFLECTIONS

Sitting in the back of the conference on race and sexuality, I realized the spectrum of concerns among the GLBT community was broader than anything filtered through the American media. Gay marriage was the tip of the iceberg. In one session alone, attendees asked about sensitivity training in senior living facilities, sex education for the GLBT handicapped, health care for the gay poor, bisexuality among teens, suicide rates, intergenerational issues, hate crimes, mentoring, and the nonlabeling trend whereby people who have sex with people of the same sex are averse to the term "gay." The mostly black and Latino audience was weary of their issues being ignored. They were not the rich white socialites paraded on TV shows for laughs, nor were they despot vampires flanking the rumor mill. But my mind kept returning to Ethan, who was conveniently removed from these contemplations with his claim that he just "wanted to be."

With the exception of our interview for this book, which resulted in his coming-out revelation, my friend Ethan and I rarely, if ever, talk about sexuality. We're not making a cultural statement, nor are we laying pride to the friendships between gay and straight communities. We are simply friends who have similar interests, who bounce around ideas about media, and who catch up with each other's lives. In writing this, I found myself asking him questions I could have answered myself. These divisive "who's straight, who's gay" questions seemed more preposterous as I went along.

To ask a gay man or lesbian woman what it's like to be gay and African American is like asking me what it's like to be black and a woman. Or asking Tiger Woods what it's like to be black and Asian. At a certain point, it's just who you are and how you express yourself. And black people are left to sift through the muck of stereotypes lining our paths to discover our individual identities.

5

SPIRITUALITY
THE NEW BLACK RELIGIOUS EXPERIENCE

A growing number of African Americans practice alternative spirituality and nontraditional Christianity.

I didn't grow up in a Baptist church. I didn't grow up AME or Pentecostal either. So I know the wealth of hymns and Negro spirituals more as historical references than because I grew up listening to them. Nor did I leave the traditional church to join the Nation of Islam.

Watching the news or even reading black publications you'd think all African Americans were fundamentalist Christians. If you're not a fundamentalist Christian or in the Nation of Islam, as far as black religious identity goes, you probably don't exist.

It's safe to say that most African Americans have parents and grandparents who emerged out of the traditional black church culture.

I was raised in a megachurch founded by a black woman in a mystical branch of Christianity called New Thought. The Bible was interpreted metaphysically, and there was a heavy emphasis on meditation, prosperous living, and the power of thought. We talked about consciousness, about names and places in the Bible symbolizing these aspects of consciousness. And Christ wasn't Jesus' last name but rather the highest state of consciousness to embody. We didn't do water baptisms, we had christenings. We didn't do communion with crackers and juice, we had spiritual communions.

Although we practiced some traditional church rudiments—we had a choir and ushers, passionate ministers, and Sunday school—we differed from conventional Christians in some very basic beliefs. For one, we didn't believe in the devil. Nor did we believe that heaven and hell were actual places but rather states of mind, because death didn't exist. Death was merely a transition from a physical to a nonphysical form. In fact, we didn't use the word "death"; we called it a "transition" instead. We had a congregation of several thousand mostly African American parishioners, and so it never dawned on me that the New Thought belief system was atypical among black people. But I was taught that everyone has his or her own path and to accept whatever spiritual journey someone chose along the way.

We had so many women ministers that I didn't know sexism was an issue in the black church. Nor did I know much about religious guilt, hell, damnation, or fire and brimstone. So when black religious leaders talk about these things, I don't have any personal experiences to relate to. I've learned to understand this rhetoric because as an African American who was raised as a Christian, albeit of a different kind, it's assumed I have some intimate knowledge of these matters. But you'd have thought when I was growing up that I wasn't Christian at all the way I was questioned by more traditional Christians on my beliefs. I had a boyfriend tell me he wouldn't marry me in my church because my minister was a woman. (Not that I wanted to marry him, but that was an insult.) I've had people ask me if I was saved and didn't know how to reply. And when I was up to it, I'd respond to the barrage of questions strangers pelted me with, giving impromptu lectures explaining the New Thought philosophy, with nothing invested in whether they got it or not.

Although I was raised in a predominantly black church that made history in its accomplishments and reach, the traditional black church as an institution I was not a part of.

But we don't have to agree. They can believe what they want; I can do the same. And we can keep bobbing around this spinning ball we call Earth and be fine.

POWER MOVES

Gray, a friend of mine, a very ambitious guy, more studious than most, suit-clad and much older in mind than the other teens during my college years, had dreams of being the next Martin Luther King. He was quite serious about it. Like many black schoolchildren, he'd been baptized in King's looming greatness and very much wanted to walk in King's shoes to uplift the community. Gray became a community organizer in high school and went to King's alma mater for college. He even got an Ivy League divinity degree before nose-diving into the work of the civil rights organizations King bred and made famous. If you wanted to be a real power broker in the black community, you had to be a minister or have some kind of divinity degree like the other leaders of the movement, he said. He mimicked King's protégés, went where they went. I'm sure he befriended them as well. After watching the wheeling and dealing of high-strung politics, the backbiting and deal making, something happened. A very grand something happened. He gave me the update over coffee at a hotel lounge.

"The masses are asses," he'd concluded. And he was taking a six-figure gig as a lobbyist for a company that embodied everything he said he stood against. It was a total 180 from his professed life's work, and I was convinced that he was merely frustrated. Maybe he was telling a joke. I couldn't be sure.

"Why won't you just start a grassroots organization?" I asked, hoping my casual reaction would be enough to juggernaut him back to his senses. I suggested that he could just work out of a church or even start one since he had divinity training, but he wasn't interested in that, either. The church just wasn't the place for him to make change, he said. Neither were these other community and civil organizations in which he'd fought so hard to rise through the ranks. So he dumped the idea of using his divinity degree for any community upliftment and focused instead on getting paid via an entity he felt had a deeper reach in black neighborhoods, a high-interest small loans company in the heart of everyone's 'hood.

His questionable morals aside, the church that historically had been the bedrock of and common-denominator experience in the black community had fast become only one of several influential factors in black life. It was no longer a requisite platform for activism. Traditionally the church had served as both the primary place for spiritual upliftment and one of the few places where African Americans could be empowered personally and politically. Segregation may dictate that a black woman could only work as a maid, but at church her dignity was restored as she led the usher board, led the deaconesses, or doubled as the church nurse. The same was true for black men, who may labor in the fields and factories, but could dress in suits, be spiritually endowed, and lead congregations. Spirituality was not some fleeting choice. In the pantheons of the black experience in America its role underscores every hallmark and progression. Faith, hope, and a rock-solid foundation in God were often all people had to remind them of their humanity in a society devoted to stripping it away. While the Christian religion was a tool used to control and justify the transatlantic slave trade, its spiritual core freed people from it. During the civil rights movement, the church served as that spiritual heart behind nonviolent protests. Not all churches, not most churches, but enough for the church and political freedom in black America to be forever linked. The influence that ministers in these churches had took on political dimensions, shaping national discussions, politics, and social agendas.

But the twentieth century was rife with dissidents taking issue with church traditions. People questioned the doctrines, the sexism, and the spin on sexuality and sin, while others questioned the very literal interpretations and their relevance in modern life. Some churches became very inclusive, tackling these issues head-on. However, people were looking for more. Some left the traditional church for other churches. Some left church for other religions. Others embarked on a spiritual quest all their own.

I think about one of my courses in grad school. The professor asked the largely African American class if they were religious. As each person answered going around the room, most were quick to note that they were not religious, but rather spiritual, in that they were not affiliated with a specific church or religion but did acknowledge a divinity in life. Had a handful of students expressed that feeling, it might not be worth mentioning. Yet nearly the entire class identified itself as spiritual. It was the beginning of the millennium, and this brash announcement was certainly a departure from, say, even a decade earlier when more traditional Christian denominations and variations of Islam in such a crowd would have been the norm. However, spirituality and a heap of self-help and other literature supporting this ideology and lifestyle were growing in mainstream exposure. More people turned to authors, lectures, television, or to themselves for spiritual identity. Not too recently, I wrote a story about an African American woman in an interracial relationship and made the mistake of mentioning that they had a shared Christian heritage. They did in fact share the same religious background, but she was steaming mad that I'd identified her as Christian. "I'm not Christian," she retorted in a heated letter. "I am spiritual." Books on spiritual identity topped the bestseller lists at the same time churches were struggling to build membership. Leadership transition from one generation to the next became a hot issue in many long-term churches. And many congregations wrestled with attracting this amorphous Gen X and Y crowd who seemed more loyal to the ideas behind church than to any church itself.

Reverend Derrick Wells, a young minister in the New Thought Christian philosophy, acknowledges the opportunities and challenges churches have today with this burgeoning spiritual identity that no longer centers around a church or any organization. "What spirituality did was it freed people from this temporal obligation that you had to do certain things." Spirituality has played a prominent role in people's growing disinterest in being controlled by institutions. People in Generation X, Gen Y, even millennials, aren't willing to be controlled in their professional lives. They will have five jobs in fifteen years, not because they aren't competent, but because they are transitory people, said Wells. Pointing to noted inspirational authors like Wayne Dyer and media icon Oprah, he says that people do not rely solely on the church for their spiritual guidance. "In the information age, the pastor's not the only one with it anymore. The shackles have been removed. I think the church is struggling with that as a new reality." Outside of a rare visit to Catholic services, Wells himself was exposed to Christianity largely through a chance CD on New Thought and reading material he stumbled upon as an adult some years after he studied Islam. The intrigue he felt led him to eventually study New Thought Christianity. But even his years studying Islam didn't tie him to a particular faith or mosque. "It was just me and a few guys in San Diego who studied together during my Navy years." It's all the more reason why the church has to reevaluate where it is, he says, but he doesn't know if the church as an institution has a great desire to do so. "The church, like most institutions, is reluctant to change. What the church has always wanted to do is change the adherence of its people instead of the church itself."

SHIFTING PARADIGMS

When Kevin Ross attended the preseminary program at Morehouse
College in the late 1990s, he was the only New Thought person
there. He worked as a chapel assistant at Martin Luther King Jr.
Chapel. "We were supposed to be ecumenical," said Ross. "But I
told the dean of chapel that we were really ecumenically Baptist."
His years there were rough. Surrounded by Christian students of
traditional denominations, he was criticized harshly. "They said I
was the devil, I was going to hell; it was awful." Even his dean described his mode of practice as "Pollyanna, positive idealists." But
Ross had a big impact on introducing the staff to New Thought phi-
losophies. Returning a decade later, Ross said the shift is amazing.
"You have atheists and Buddhists who work as chapel assistants
now," he said.

Ross notes that there are churches making fundamental changes
in how they reach their congregations. The advent of technology
is one difference. "Many people are going to church by watching
television or watching podcasts," said Ross, who thinks it's a good
thing. Many churches offer webcasts and webinars of their services
and workshops. People can watch and pay tithes online. Reverend
T. D. Jakes's chapel is set up so that people can plug in their laptops
and ask questions via the Internet that he can respond to, he says.
And there are other innovations. "I can show you some churches
that would blow your mind." Pointing to white right-winger Rick
Warren, Ross notes, "He has a Starbucks on his campus and TVs
there for people who simply want to go to church, but they don't
want to go to church. You can go there in your Bermuda shorts, get
your coffee, and put your tithe in and leave." Ross believes "the
church is beginning to respond to this audience," explaining how in

"the children's church, you walk in and it's a spiritual Disney World. In the youth ministry, they have video games you can play before service. They have a skateboard ramp outside the youth ministry."

Innovation aside, I wondered, with this shifting relationship between the church and African Americans, what impact will this evolution have on the church's ability to be an organizing centrifuge? Will the attributed political clout of being a minister in the black community dissipate? Has it already dissipated? "The social change that's associated with our churches isn't evident in these avenues," Ross says, referring to the nonchurchgoing, spiritualist crowd. "You're not going to get that from watching Joel Olsteen on TV or reading Iyanla Vanzant. However, these individuals do a better job of meeting this nonchurch community where they are."

Recalling President Obama's highly publicized split from Jeremiah Wright, whose politicized sermons made national headlines during the primaries in 2008, it was evident that cameras were peering into a world that had typically been media-proof. Never before had the political nature of black theology, a hybrid of Christianity and branches of black nationalism, been shoved up sound-bite style on a world stage. It was a first. Whether the media hype that forged the split was justified or not, one thing is evident: the first African American president of the United States, a self-professed Christian, is not affiliated with a church that facilitated his rise or can capitalize from it. Obama reportedly has spiritual advisers. Has the time come when a black church affiliation, which used to catapult African American leaders to fame, can become a liability? The implications of that question alone underscore a changing of the times.

SPIRITUALISTS

Kemba N'Namdi didn't go to church as a child in Detroit. Her parents were raised Episcopalian and Catholic. While they wanted their children to know spirituality, they didn't want them entangled in church institutions. "We grew up following the laws of the universe," said N'Namdi. "It's more understandable to people today because you have the book *The Secret*. But growing up it was so not popular."

Rather than attend religious services, N'Namdi's family had group discussions about spirituality and were given books to read. "We read *Science of the Mind* by Ernest Holmes or *Love Is Letting Go of Fear*," she recalls. But N'Namdi was always familiar with the range of religions. "Growing up I was exposed to so many different people in different religions. The first Jews I knew were African American. The first Muslims, the first Buddhists, were African American."

Although she's felt pressure to identify herself along religious lines, N'Namdi says Universalist is probably the best label she can find, and even that's not accurate. She attends a spiritual institution that quotes from all the major religious texts.

"I'll tell my mom, I didn't grow up Episcopalian. I didn't grow up Christian. I read the Bible on my own, after I read the Koran and the Torah. But I'm not coming from these teachings that have been instilled in me. I didn't get any of that."

Jonathan Woods was raised Baptist by Southern-reared parents. But he always wondered if there was more. While attending a progressive Baptist church that emphasized African traditions, his pastor, who'd studied Egyptology, asked if he'd ever explored other religions. "How do you know this is it for you?" the pastor asked him. Woods had already begun reading books on African religions.

Soon after the query he got down on his knees, prayed to God, and asked that he know what Jesus knew. Instantly, he was led to the Medu Neter, the text for an Egyptian spirituality–based organization. "I felt like all of these questions I had were being answered. Other people thought the way I did, and they were part of a society that lasted for centuries." Woods and several friends took classes on the book. They wrote poetry about their revelations, and people who heard their poetry at various settings enrolled in classes as well. A flock of students enrolled and began a cross-religious comparison. Using the book as a basis, the students went on their own individual paths of study. "Some started really studying Hinduism or yoga. Others got into the martial arts and Chinese arts. Others just started contemplating, and that's where I wound up." As part of Woods's practice, he does a sunrise salutation in the morning, talks to the ancestors at night, and is a practicing vegetarian.

AFRICAN TRADITIONS

"My parents were churched out by the time I came along," says Mariahdessa Ekere Tallie, a Queens-reared poet. Her grandmother was a Pentecostal preacher with a church in upstate New York. Her parents were raised Pentecostal, but Tallie wasn't exposed to any of it as a child. "We only went to church on Easter. My sister was a Jehovah's Witness. My babysitter was Catholic, and I would go with her to confession; I liked the idea of confession," she says. On occasion, her mom would take her to meditation classes. Many of Tallie's teenage friends turned to Islam for spiritual guidance. Tallie began a quest all her own. She decided she wanted to practice an African traditional religion. "Something we did before colonization," she said. While a freshman at Clark Atlanta University, she studied Egyptian practices, then someone introduced her to the Yoruba orishas. "The orisha community isn't one you just access," she said. She came across some practitioners at an African street festival in Atlanta. Later she took an African women's studies class at Morris Brown College and discovered that her professor practiced Yoruba. Years later, she was officially initiated.

The Yoruba religion celebrates one god, and the orishas are nature-based aspects of that god. Homage to ancestors is a major component of the practice, and Tallie set aside an altar in their honor. She meditates and prays daily. Some days she prays holding various orishas in her consciousness. "Sometimes I go to orisha dance classes. Singing and dancing are also forms of prayer," she says. While she has a lot of artistic renderings of various orishas in her house, she also notes that she has a Buddha statue and books on Native American spirituality. Although she's embraced Yoruba, she's very respectful of Christianity and the role it played in her ancestors' lives. She keeps a cross and Bible on her altar in honor of her ancestors as well. "I considered going to church this Christmas," she said. "I feel a connection to my lineage through that as well." Although she doesn't typically celebrate Christmas, she does celebrate the winter solstice, the ancient, indigenous celebration that Christmas was later designated to replace.

However, Tallie takes issue with the way African traditional religions are misrepresented in the media. "They act like we're just killing chickens and there's all this insanity going on. There's a prejudice against anything African and African spirituality. It's fear. Even black folks don't get it. My own dad didn't get it." Tallie finds much of the skepticism among African Americans ironic, saying that the orishas are always around. "I do laugh because they have symbols of the religion around their house and don't even know it. I have an aunt who has a huge statue of an orisha, high up. I asked her, 'What are you doing with that picture up there?' She said she just liked it. But she had it in the right place. You go to people's houses and they have collections of sea shells or certain color schemes, and I'm thinking, *You're dealing with orisha energy and don't even know it.* My mom has a huge collection of sea shells and rocks and coral and tons of stuff from the sea that evoke Iemoja."

Tallie is raising her two young children as Yoruba, but she's accepted that they may choose different paths, too. And she's taken them to Hindu temples and Native American powwows to expose them to other forms of spirituality.

PATH TO BUDDHAHOOD

When Vikki Ewing came home during her freshman year proudly sporting her Spelman College sweatshirt, her father, a leader in the Buddhist community, was taken aback by the inscription "Our school for Christ" emblazoned on the school crest. "What is that about?" he demanded. Nor did he understand why she was required to take two Christian-based religion courses, including The History of the Black Church.

"I want to see if there's anything else that would be more beneficial for my life," said Ewing. Although she attended churches and went to church school after college, she didn't feel a deep, spiritual connection, and she reestablished her Buddhist faith.

Ewing grew up in a Buddhist household where chanting in the morning and evening was as familiar as soul food dinner. Her parents were introduced to Buddhism while students in college during the 1960s, and the experience saved their union and changed their lives. But as a child, Ewing was always apprehensive about sharing her spiritual beliefs with others. "It was really hard," she said, recounting the stories of traditional Christians who challenged her. "I didn't want to hear that I was a devil worshiper." And she hesitated to invite friends over who would witness her family chanting.

But the African American Buddhist community is a large one. "It's so much larger than people would imagine. When you say Buddhism, people think Asian. But there is a very large African American Buddhist population," she says, noting that she sees a burgeoning group of blacks under forty turning to the faith.

But people do assume that because she's black, she's also Christian. "Let's say I'm at a social setting or at a sorority function, they'll have a prayer and will assume that everyone prays to God." She also had run-ins with boyfriends who insisted that they wanted a Christian wife.

But sharing her faith has become much easier over the years, despite the fact that few people associate Buddhism with African Americans. "Outside of the Tina Turner *What's Love Got to Do with It?* movie, I don't know if you've ever seen African Americans as Buddhist in the media," Ewing says. The mother of two young boys, she's raising them as Buddhist, too.

"All religions have their similarities," she says. "It's all about which path is best for you."

TEXAS REVISITED

My grandfather passed recently. A hardworking, Texas-born man who could fix just about anything, he'd raised my dad, aunt, and uncle—all became college grads—in a small town just south of Houston. A church mainstay, he dedicated much of his later life to a small African Methodist Episcopal (AME) church. I was surprised to discover that he taught Sunday school and Bible studies, not to mention functioned as the church handyman for most of his pseudo-retirement years. The church was modest, nearly a century old, and had survived many a hurricane in its day. It was a hauntingly familiar place. My other grandfather had also sat in its pews, as well as my grandmothers. It was here where they chose to raise their children. The minister was a middle-aged woman. Her assistants were women as well, a dramatic departure, I'm sure, from the town's past. The church was too small to hold my grandfather's funeral there, so the service was conducted a few blocks away at another familiar church, the site of my aunt's wedding. And listening to the sermons, whose language was such a departure from what I was more familiar with, I thought about Mariahdessa Ekere Tallie and her appreciation for the role traditions had played in her family despite her decision to embrace another path. With all the beauty and history housed in these institutions, I wondered how the past would bridge with the future, with the new lifestyles.

6

THE HIP-HOP FACTOR
BLACK ART IN A COMMERCIAL LANDSCAPE

Emerging African American artists are shaped but not limited by the dominance and impact of hip-hop music and culture.

Hip-hop juggernauted into the arts scene like a hail of firecrackers at an opera. But there's no denying that hip-hop and its commercialized cousins demanded the attention. Raw, urgent, controversial, and street, it transcended New York City fad status to become a global, billion-dollar industry all its own. While the five-pronged culture—an amalgamation of breakers, MCs, DJs, graffiti, and gritty fashion—emerged from a cool-kids scene of underground trekkers in the early 1980s, by the turn of the century it was the soundtrack for champagne sippers and tastemakers, and nearly a decade later hip-hop has become an American staple: bona fide, rubber-stamped pop. Although throngs of brown men and women made plush livings forging the art of rhyme and break beats, millions more embraced the music as their new-school mantra, a mic for young America—with we-are-the-world aspirations, movin'-on-up ethos, and some extra machismo for take-charge's sake.

I've loved hip-hop; I've hated hip-hop. The hypocrisies and hypermasculinity all too often shadowed the innovation, and fans who loved the art form's battle cry for freedom and authenticity had a hard time wrestling with the art form's commercial turn.

Being a living witness to hip-hop's evolution has been as amusing as it's been confusing.

At its best, men and women wield words like political daggers. Hip-hop embodies a verbal ray of hope that makes poetry breathe again. At its worst, hip-hop fans the flames of unyielding ignorance, misogyny, and racial stereotypes.

Everyone who is anyone in the black Gen X demo has an in-depth opinion on hip-hop and its stepchild, gangsta rap. If you don't, well, you just don't exist. We've been dubbed the hip-hop generation when we're not being hyperanalyzed as Generation X and Y. And young black America, for better or worse, has been viewed by the world through the distorted prism of rap's pop standards.

If you were an artist who came of age in the last three decades, there was no escaping hip-hop's looming presence. Love it or hate it, or be you sandwiched in between, you can't dispute the music was the adrenaline rush pumping through the veins of young America. It ruptured cracks in city sidewalks, shook the windows of our Cape Cod homes, kept us moving and grooving and hyper-happy and blazing mad. Although some tried in vain to resist the commercial ways of the hip-hop world, we wanted all its platinum-draped trappings of the American dream supersized, microwaved, and to go.

What began for me as a dancer's fascination with backspin dreams quickly became a lifelong talking point for cultural relevance. Blame it on *VIBE* magazine. A big-haired freshman at Clark Atlanta University, I discovered the mag in my freshman-week goodie bag and was struck by the reality that I could document this bubbling art form's innovators and controversies, triumphs and tragedies, to help others understand themselves. A music lover with a serious anthropologist bent, I adopted the mission, peering through a microscope into the underbelly of a culture I hoped would hold the keys to who we were.

I've juggled the double duty of defending and critiquing the genre. I've wrestled its well-worn lyrics to the ground, bled from its verbal assaults, defended its right to breathe, and lay hypnotized by the sheer force of the influence and controversy of talented men and women who just wanted to be heard. I've covered hip-hop's artists, stood in awe of its cultural prowess, and was ultimately moved by the entrepreneurial spirit embraced by 'hood-reared talents who were unusually candid about their business acumen.

I knew a change was coming as early as the seventh grade when Public Enemy's "Fight the Power" hit the airwaves. When people rap in berets with foot soldiers behind them with banners of black heroes and sheroes on pop music stations, surely that's indicative of a shift.

■ ■ ■

Little did I know that that change would be caused by money. Not money to forge a sweeping end to poverty or usher in major reforms, but rather big money as an aspirational possibility for anyone in hip-hop's blazing path. The dream had been sold. You could become a millionaire if you walked the hip-hop way, or so it seemed, a mode that included unabashed do-you posturing with unapologetically bold actions while being yourself. Dream big, think big was pushed on airwaves, and listeners invested their faith in that half-full reality with reckless abandon. Call it a mentality shift for many urban kids, but the possibility of being the next Donald Trump suddenly seemed very feasible, particularly if the possibility was underscored by a driving bass line and a diamond-studded earring to match. When P. Diddy in all his swag made Cristal the new tap water and 50 Cent liquidated a Vitamin Water investment into $400 million, the conversation about art for art's sake in hip-hop became increasingly difficult to hold.

This isn't to say the art of hip-hop totally dissipated or that fans weren't emotionally invested in its success. People argued over which rapper was the best. Who was the better lyricist was test question numero uno in barbershop arguments, a four-way tie between Tupac, Biggie, Rakim, and Jay-Z, with Lil Wayne thrown in on occasion. But who was better didn't usurp who was the most paid (Jay-Z), or who made the best business moves (Jay-Z), or who had the best investment portfolio (Jay-Z again).

What did change was that few people, if any, were rapping for rap's sake. Whereas a woman with a decent voice may be content to work a nine-to-five and sing in the church choir, no one, and I mean no one, with any proverbial rap skills was content with "rapped on the side." The days of the B-boy kids on the corner who wanted to be the best on the block became a relic of hip-hop's golden past. People with the gift of rhyme now wanted six-figure deals. From the studio basement to the big time.

But everyone wasn't peachy cool with hip-hop's dominance, especially other artists who weren't rappers and had another message to share. Hip-hop's biggest critics deplored the sexual and often violent lyrics, the risqué music videos, the mounting criminal records of A-list rappers. All that was wrong with black America was hand-pumped by hip-hop, argued critics. Every crime in urban America was supposedly caused by rap's unruliness. Even hip-hop fashion was single-handedly blamed for the emasculation of men in the 'hood, particularly those sagging pants, which several small-town politicos now ban and fine people for wearing.

But it was the authenticity argument that drove artists up the padded walls of insanity. Historically, black music and art were praised for their ability to reflect the purity in human emotion. Aretha Franklin's wail, Romare Bearden's strokes, Langston Hughes's words, all painting pictures of beauty and honor where others saw pain and despair. There was a nobility in their desire to capture these worlds and a time-respected responsibility to forever remind society that the nation's downtrodden were human, too.

Today some argue that, for better or worse, hip-hop now plays the role of that authentic voice from the world of the otherwise unknown and unseen. Others challenge that the art form was co-opted by moneymaking interests long ago and is as real as the plastic button on the remote that critics use to turn it off.

MONEY, MONEY, MONEY

The dichotomy of hip-hop's promise versus its moneymaking realities permeated the art scene. Spoken word, whose American roots lie in the protest poetry of the 1960s, was on the upswing in the mid-1990s. A close cousin to rap, spoken word's popularity soared as rap's did. Its resurrection was christened in the movie *Love Jones* in 1997 and by Russell Simmons's launch of Def Poetry Jam in 2005. Spoken word, unlike other poetry, specifically explored social consciousness, love, and eroticism and did so in an oratorical style similar to Baptist preaching. The rhyme scheme in spoken word was identical to the range of poetry styles taught in English class with some verbal acrobatics thrown in as well. Hip-hop in both the purist form and so-called gangsta variations explored 'hood life from its aspirations to day-to-day musings and problems, or some twisted fantasy version of all three. As hip-hop fans grew weary of the rising materialism and street-life stories, they turned to the spoken-word portals for a breather.

Spoken-word nights are as common as club nights in some cities. No longer relegated to college campuses, spoken word is a lively art form with devout audiences and creators.

Khari "Discopoet" B, the son of a jazz artist and spoken-word poet in Chicago, has led his discopoetry events for nearly a decade.

Much like rappers, poets are also tagged for a variation of street credibility. "We're expected to live what we speak," said Khari. "You're looked at as a preacher so there's supposed to be a greater responsibility behind your actions. If you're an erotic poet, you're expected to put your leg behind your head, swing from the ceiling fan, and if you can't do that you're wack. Or if I'm doing all this revolutionary poetry—save the children, fight the man—then when I'm not onstage, I'm expected to be working with some children's program, or not running when the sirens come. And I think that's good. It separates the mice from the men."

Immersed in the scene while studying at Tennessee State University, the engineering major switched course and has trod the path of truth-spewing ever since. A ball of kinetic energy, Khari uses live soul bands reminiscent of funk as the backdrop for his fireball political poetry. Khari leads the charge for poetry largely to counter the commercialism of the independent black voice.

"Poetry is saying the things that hip-hop used to say," he says. "We speak to that contingency of people who don't want to do what the masses are doing. I have to remind people of the limitless strength they have as people."

Referring to the early years of jazz and the black arts movements of the 1950s through the 1970s, he says, "Our voice was our voice; it wasn't so co-opted for commercial use. There were no commercials selling Downy with the Black Panthers. Martin Luther King wasn't hustling toilet tissue. Hip-hop, which was the continuation of that voice, got sanitized."

But even this commitment to noncommercialism became difficult as the financial stakes for hip-hop artists soared.

Many neighborhood poets weren't satisfied with an open mic here and there to inspire the masses. Even a self-published book or professorship seemed too modest a goal. Instead, new-school poets wanted greasy record deals, the same record deals they often chastised as selling out in poetry haunts.

So while spoken word's popularity was a flip side to hip-hop's mainstreaming, the poetry world, too, fell victim to the prospects of fame. "Poetry hasn't maintained its integrity, and it's not going to," Khari says. "Like rock 'n' roll, like blues, the money came in, and there are people who see that as their only option to make it out. It's OK. People want their fifteen minutes of fame; they want to say they were seen by this many people, so they'll be willing to pacify their art to make it happen. That's not everybody. There will always be an underground, people who may or may not want that same fame, but they're not willing to negotiate."

But the art scene at large got caught up in the hip-hop frenzy.

Jazz musicians who at varying points stuck a middle finger to hip-hop's musical viability and posted a screw-you sentiment to its use of tracks over musicians soon slipped rap samples and mimicked break beats into their shows. Even R & B had to become hip-hop to survive, and the neo-soul movement of the late 1990s positioned itself as the ideological antithesis to rap's materialistic values. Classically trained dancers mastered hip-hop to become background dancers. Taggers who once raised the ire of politicians nationwide moved from public nuisance to museum-worthy innovators.

THE BLACK TEST

Jumaane N'Namdi runs G. R. N'Namdi Art Gallery, a premiere abstract art gallery of artists of the African diaspora in Chicago, Detroit, and New York. One of his consummate beefs with the trials of black art is the belief that African American artists are required to prove their cultural merit by making some overt statement about identity and race. "It's expected," says N'Namdi. "Black artists are expected to discuss race and the hardships they experience as a result of it. In some competitive scenes, that's all they want to hear." It's not good enough, for example, to paint an aesthetically pleasing flower. You have to link this flower to racism, degradation, slavery, colonialism, powerlessness.

You get the picture.

"Look, if you're doing a contemporary piece and you're making some personal commentary on race as you've experienced it, fine, but everyone's not doing that. They're pulling on old imagery and trigger words to jolt a reaction, which ultimately takes away from the work."

During the Harlem Renaissance and the black arts movement, there were black theorists who believed black artists should create work about the black struggle and the journey of the black community. "Every avenue that was available to us had to be focused on civil rights and increasing the visibility of black people on an academic and political scale," said Nathaniel Quinn, a professor and renowned artist whose abstract works appear across the nation. But today there is not that kind of cohesive thought about how to attain equal rights, says Quinn. "Today is heavily based on products, merchandising, fashion, and music. It's not based on black artists' feeling they have to make work to achieve equal rights for black people. We don't feel that kind of pressure now. We can't fathom that kind of pressure now."

While black artists have more freedom of expression, the expectation to at least comment on race is standard. "If your work is completely absent, with no reference to black identity, then you'll have a hard time," he says.

Rhonda Wheatley knows this well. Her art explores language, including elements of Sanskrit and African texts.

But when she showed her work to curators at a space in New York City, they refused to showcase it, stating that they only showcased work that discussed black identity. "Race is just one form of identity," she says. "Of course that's something we struggled for. In my work I talk about how language is this limited range of thoughts and how other cultures have words for things we don't. So when I was stretching these words, it was really about stretching my think-ing, and that's beyond my cultural background."

"Should I have to feel that because I'm black I have to do my art about blackness?" she ponders. "I would say that too many black folks have struggled and fought so that I can do art about what I want to do."

■ ■ ■

"Hip-hop has had a tremendous influence both positively and nega-tively in my art and my life," said Leon Q, a Chicago-reared Latin jazz trumpet player in his twenties. Leon's forays into jazz ultimate-ly led him to embrace salsa, samba, and the world of Latin music. He's traveled the world, fronts an Afro-Cuban band, and writes his own music. However, he's constantly being questioned by other African Americans for his enthusiasm for Latin music:

> People look at me funny. They ask me, well, why aren't you doing R & B and hip-hop? Most people feel that black music only encompasses R & B, hip-hop, jazz. It's my obligation to educate people on those new concepts so they can see the vast expan-siveness of music. When people talk about black music, particularly here in America, our scope of what black music is is very narrow. Black music is world music. Every music you can possibly find has been influenced by black music. They look at me and say he's a black guy who does salsa. But the people who made that music were black people just like us. Not African Americans.

■ ■ ■

Are the artistic merits of today's artists tied to their hip-hop savvy? Are emerging African American poets, musicians, singers, and painters now pigeonholed between a cultural rusty pocketknife and a brandished .45 revolver, either being rated by the success of their hip-hop luminaries and proving their hip-hop credibility or else feeling compelled to berate the one global phenomenon of their culture?

I wonder if hip-hop is now a black-consciousness litmus test, a de facto common denominator for black innovators with a voice. Hip-hop is often the world through which their art is funneled, the yardstick for its relevance, and the line in the sand for artistic consciousness.

I AM HIP-HOP

Nearly every artist I spoke with between the ages of eighteen and forty-five admitted that hip-hop had some impact on their work. Whether obvious or subtle, both an acknowledgment of the far-reaching impact of hip-hop and a desire to identify with it were particularly strong, especially among men.

Quinn, an NYU grad and painter in his thirties whose work has graced the walls of the Rush Arts Gallery and the Brooklyn Museum of Art, among others, has explored both identity and fashion in his work. But the Brooklyn resident now exclusively reconstructs masculine and feminine images in hip-hop.

"What else would I paint about?" he asks. "Today's culture is so governed and mobilized by hip-hop culture. A lot of the images you see in mainstream media are based on hip-hop, and being a contemporary artist, I have this duty to make paintings on the contemporary culture in which I live."

His latest exploration, a look at the "tender warrior," is an ode to the balance between masculinity and femininity in leading hip-hop stars.

"You have these African American men who are portrayed in ways that are hypermasculine, but they're also tender and vulnerable," he says. "TI has that song that goes, 'You can have whatever you like.' Here's a guy from the South posing himself as this real assertive, very masculine character. It's a very masculine thing to provide financial security for a woman, and that's made very clear in the video. But then there are these scenes in the video where he's giving her a candlelight dinner, he's taking her to these romantic places. He's taking her to this beach spot and looking at her in an admirable way. In that sense he's romantic."

■ ■ ■

John Jennings, an assistant professor at the University of Illinois, teaches hip-hop design. "It's such a unique way of presenting material and requires study," said Jennings. A hip-hop head as a teen, Jennings is dedicated to teaching the core design elements of hip-hop and tracking its evolution. The curator of an exhibit on black comic books, Jennings argues that hip-hop's influence in the design world has gone global. He's a big advocate of media education, utilizing hip-hop as a tool. "We live in an age dominated by media, and drawing that line between what we see in pictures and reality can be very difficult without the proper framework." With consumerism at an all-time high, the co-opting of images that feel real for other purposes can be particularly confusing, he says. "Hip-hop, an amalgamation of imagery and words, is similar to comics and can be an excellent tool for helping to deconstruct this imagery." But Jennings's studies pull from the aesthetic of hip-hop to understand the commercial versions and media images today. He, too, takes issue with the commercial aspects, but notes, "That's how cultures in capitalist societies work. A cultural phenomenon unfolds, then it's snatched up and sold back to you in a self-contained way that seems familiar, yet it's foreign. We embrace it, form a new culture to substantiate it, and then a subculture emerges and it happens all over again." A study of hip-hop is the perfect platform to understand those relationships, he argues.

But he asserts that he is very much hip-hop. "I consider myself to be a hip-hop artist because I advocate for the culture. There's no way for me to be an artist in this generation without having the experience of hip-hop. The culture of hip-hop has to do with the MC, the DJ, the tagger, the B-boy. If you go to one of those artistic avenues to represent hip-hop, it doesn't matter where you come from, the lifestyle you live, it doesn't matter what your social views are, all it states is that you're an advocate of the culture. The viewpoint of being an advocate of the culture has to be expanded." But the art form has had dueling effects on his life. "The positive impact is that it gave me room to expand in how I express myself musically. Speaking in syntax, arranging their words over a rhythm . . . without having to go the traditional route of singing or playing an instrument. Negatively, hip-hop, being the largest genre of music in the world, it has lent itself to a lot of generalities."

■ ■ ■

While Wheatley had never thought about hip-hop's effect on her work, even she admitted that her pieces are reminiscent of graffiti art. "I've been inspired by graffiti and these word distortions. Hip-hop as a culture is very postmodern in the way they pull snippets from everywhere. In the music there's sampling, pulling from several different places, and relabeling it. In that sense, when I collage and layer my work, I'm taking something from different places and layering it." Despite this, she doesn't think anyone would look at her work and think hip-hop.

"Graffiti is very male dominated. I love to see beauty graffiti. It's rebellious. The hard edge is literally the curves in the letter. I have these soft, flowing lines. I'm probably more influenced by hip-hop than I thought. I have an affinity to rappers in changing the sounds and words. We have things in common; I think, also, I just avoid labels. I wouldn't say I'm doing hip-hop. I can have a conversation and show commonalities, but to take on this label would exclude all other influences."

BLACK ENTREPRENEURS
NEW URBAN IMPRESARIOS
AND POSTRACIAL SHOPKEEPERS

African American entrepreneurs forge new paths as they cultivate fresh markets and untapped opportunities.

A few years back, when I was hot on the trail of every ethnic marketing seminar with a press release that flew across my desk, I kept bumping into this urban-versus-black conversation. It was a hot argument indeed, rife with verbal sparring, word splitting, and theories ideal for the *Harvard Business Review*. Up until nearly a decade ago, tossing around the terms "African American" and "urban market" was like talking about two peas in a pod. Any marketer worth his or her salt knew that "urban" was code for the black audience. And the never-ending battle to determine how best to reach this market, how to leverage black media and black ad agencies to capture this market, and how to harness the collective power of black consumers was documented to no end. The quest seemed to be how best to convince mainstream companies to allocate more dollars toward effectively reaching the African American consumer, who for decades was undervalued. Too many companies were content to utilize their general marketing campaigns to reach the black audience. Whereas African Americans may support various products and companies, such companies didn't always reinvest in African American communities.

The "new urban" moniker was kicked into vogue and paralleled hip-hop's premillennium commercial takeover. A few savvy marketers noticed the highly multicultural trendsetter crowd, heavily influenced by African American consumers, and positioned their products to reach them. From fashion to tech gadgets, media to automobiles, urban goods spoke to a youth-fueled lifestyle that companies wanted to project.

VIBE magazine's first publishers, Keith Clinkscale and Len Burnett, were the biggest proponents of the new urban definition. "Urban" didn't mean just the African American audience; it included upwardly mobile and young hipster white, Latino, and Asian consumers whose shared hip-hop lifeline had cultivated a lifestyle and culture all its own. It was also a sleek way of cracking the black-world box, so to speak, and of appealing to advertisers who might think twice about targeting an African American audience but were intrigued by the sex appeal of this multicultural audience. The new urban label was a smart way to sell products typically aimed at black audiences to a more expansive clientele. This new urban audience enabled businesses to dance around the limits of race relations and reemphasize youth culture. So it comes as no surprise that music, with its transnational appeal, became the surfboard of choice for many budding entrepreneurs looking for that tidal wave of monetary success. While Berry Gordy's Motown model of crossover success predated hip-hop by thirty years, and the notion of crossover appeal has in fact existed since pop music hit the charts, the changing times enabled music-business visionaries ushering in the new millennium to launch a number of affiliated black-owned businesses that capitalized on the music culture.

Def Jam cofounder Russell Simmons laid the framework for hip-hop impresarios and others to follow. Simmons launched a series of ventures including Phat Farm, a multimillion-dollar fashion empire; the Prepaid Visa RushCard; and the Hip-Hop Summit Action Network, a nonprofit financial education tool. Each venture centered around his success leading a pioneering record label and leveraged his incredible sense of what appeals to this new urban market. Simmons doesn't get much credit for inspiring a generation of entrepreneurs. But he should. He is indisputably a prototype for a new model of entrepreneurship, baseball cap and all. His financial and political education efforts show his awareness of his influence not just culturally but as a model for leadership in business.

■ ■ ■

No one, however—in the music world at least—embodied this new urban mix of champagne-popping, aspirational urban chic more than P. Diddy himself.

Diddy, an underrated marketing genius, became a one-man selling machine for all things "urban refined." While Diddy gets hated on for any number of reasons, he personifies new urban and all the conflicting oxymorons that give it life. He's worldly and 'hood, educated and street smart, flashy and streamlined, and he juggles it all like a masterful ringleader heading a star-studded circus. And it's Diddy's "you can do it all: headline on Broadway, run a marathon, lead a fashion empire, run a label, be the star artist— among other pastimes" example that's got millions of goal-setting Gen Xers and Yers working like maniacs. Diddy's "don't stop, won't stop, do you" edict is intoxicating to the young entrepreneur–mini mogul in training.

■ ■ ■

I ran the notion of Simmons and Diddy breathing new life into the prospects of entrepreneurship and the collective vein of black-owned businesses by some entrepreneur friends of mine, and they agreed that the hip-hop impresarios did just that.

"But you're forgetting someone," a friend of mine said.

"Who's that?" I asked.

"Michael Jordan," he said. "Michael Jordan is hip-hop. Everything Puffy's done, Michael already did. Mike partnered with Bob Johnson. Look at Russell and look at Puffy. He did everything that Puffy did without the flair. He smoked cigars before everyone. He listened to smooth stuff, but what do you think they play in the locker room? You need to listen to something hyped. He's in a cold-ass town, cold-ass city. He's on this sorry-ass team; of course he was listening to hip-hop. He needed something to keep him sane."

Not that I needed to be convinced. M.J.'s name alone is synonymous with success. His brand was platinum when everyone was rocking gold. Nike became a Fortune 100 company thanks to M.J.'s brand power. His ability to endorse anything and make it a global must-have was mind-blowing. His integrity, drive, pure sports smarts, and clean-cut-with-swag image redefined the NBA, sports, and the sheer power of urban marketing in the mid-1980s before there was such a thing as urban marketing. As for the new urban context, M.J.'s fashion brands in particular balanced urban sophistication and worldly, refined class. Air Jordans and the Team Jordan fashion lines became global status symbols. While I'd never thought about M.J. in the hip-hop or urban marketing context, the whole black and red shoes, baggy shorts, tongue wagging, and by-any-means-necessary approach to the game was very much so. His ability to create teams and leverage that success into an array of highly profitable albeit quiet business deals centered around his brand was legendary and was very hip-hop impresario without the baggage of language to define it. He had sports apparel, a basketball team, endorsement deals, and a record label among his numerous ventures. M.J. was his own brand in the same way that Mercedes, Microsoft, and Reebok were, for that matter. Everyone, not just aspiring black entrepreneurs, wanted to be like Mike.

■ ■ ■

I'd be remiss if I didn't mention that many African Americans in the business community become highly annoyed when black people in sports and entertainment are held up as examples of stellar businesspersons. It's no accident that it's much easier for an African American rapper starting, say, a dog kennel to get more media attention and financing opportunities for his flight of fancy than an experienced, expert, but unknown African American dog trainer and kennel owner to do so. If it weren't for publications like *Black Enterprise* and *New Vision in Business* the black business owners who aren't famous via their entertainment pursuits wouldn't be covered at all. Nevertheless, M.J., Simmons, and Diddy changed the game.

■ ■ ■

Those who opposed this multicultural take on the urban tag argued that it would ultimately dilute the power of the African American market. The argument went that companies and advertisers would avoid targeting the black consumer as a whole in favor of this expanded urban market. The new urban had a heavy trendsetter component that didn't include the entire African American market. Moreover, products designed specifically for African American consumers that didn't have this cool hip-hop factor couldn't dovetail off the new urban appeal. It was especially complicated for black-owned publications and black ad agencies, whose African American audiences spanned the gamut of age groups, lifestyles, and interests. Once the new urban became more inclusive, black-owned media and agencies could lose their edge in their main argument: that *they* were the best way to reach the black audience.

The new urban was riding high into the 2Ks, and a number of African American businesses, particularly in retail, the service sector, marketing, and fashion, were able to forge a life under its banner. Then something totally predictable happened that sideswiped those overachievers.

New urban went general market.

Just like those fashions in Italian *Vogue* eventually filter into the affordable everyman reach of discount retail stores across America, new urban, too, expanded its reach. New urban no longer centered around African American tastemakers as consumers, entrepreneurs, or innovators in the culture. New urban could be general market with urban frills. The fears of the anti–new urban critics were somewhat confirmed: when black magazines with the new urban moniker went to Advertiser X execs to convince them they could reach the coveted urban audience through their magazine, they were increasingly told they weren't needed to access an audience that was now as white as it was black. "Can't we reach them in *GQ*?" advertisers asked.

BACK TO BLACK

Tyler Perry, another one-man marketing machine, who catapulted his touring theater fame into box office and TV success, flew totally under the radar during this transformation of new urban. Perry cultivated an all-ages African American market whose modest lifestyles didn't fit into the new urban box. He launched a series of comedies with strong family themes. His domestic box office numbers were astounding. And conventional wisdom was dumbfounded. But he underscored what many African American marketing experts had been chanting for years, that black audiences can be successfully reached via effective target marketing.

So when new urban went mainstream, urban went back to black. And the terms became interchangeable again.

This became obvious at a recent conference I attended for African American magazines. When I asked the panelists to describe the difference between new urban and urban, they danced around the answer. They viewed multicultural marketing as general marketing. The debate that enlivened discussions a decade ago was long gone. There was no difference. As far as these panelists were concerned urban meant black, and the fight for advertisers in the 2009 recession was harder than it had ever been.

THE POSTRACIAL SHOPKEEPERS

Although new urban didn't level the playing field in black media, it did something equally as interesting. The new urban concept launched a wave of businesses by African American entrepreneurs that targeted a combination of multiracial and African American aspirational consumers.

Traditionally, black business owners were pegged in one of two extremes: either you had a black-owned business in a black neighborhood that had a black audience or, more recently, you owned a company targeting the general market in which cultural identity was not relevant to the product or service. The former was easier than the latter. But the hip-hop impresario allowed the possibility for both. Entrepreneurs could take a product or service and reach a multicultural audience while retaining aspects of African American culture in their product and marketing.

The following businesses share a story. Each breaks the mode of the traditional African American entrepreneur. Each business is highly influenced by African American culture. Each business is black-owned. None is based in a black neighborhood. Each owner uses avenues in black media to promote his or her product; however, they're heavily reliant on Internet marketing. And finally, but most striking, the audience for their product is not specifically black.

None of these businesses or their success should be shocking if you've been following trends for the past few years. These entrepreneurs are among thousands who are forging a new identity for black business owners.

The Jeweler

I like the Silver Room. It's a funky jewelry shop nestled in Chicago's Wicker Park neighborhood. Thrift store chic has also gone mainstream, and the Silver Room is one of the few shops I've found that doesn't have overpriced, dime-a-dozen trinkets I could have picked up in Atlanta's Little Five Points during my college days. But that's another story. Eric Williams opened the Silver Room in 1997. The eclectic shop has an array of unique jewelry, ornate crystals, and silver Williams picks up on his travels to Japan, East Africa, Israel, and Mexico. He showcases local designers, too. The Silver Room is a mainstay in Wicker Park, an ethnically diverse neighborhood that used to house more artists than yuppies, with a host of tastemaker bars, record shops, and vintage hocks. Raised in Chicago's south suburbs, Williams saw his dad run a neighborhood bar as a kid and was bit by the entrepreneurship bug early on. He reasons that his shop wouldn't do well in an all-black area; nor would it do well in an all-white area. His shoppers are definitively urban, multiracial trendsetters who want some edge in their wrist- and neckwear.

He markets through his e-mail database and by hosting a series of arts-centered events that cater to his audience. Prices range from ten dollars to the upper hundreds.

The Shoe Store

Ernel Dawkins, a former schoolteacher, launched Laced Up in 2005. I met Dawkins at a celebrity-laden *King* magazine promotional event he hosted at his store. An Atlanta-based sneaker boutique, Laced Up services the sneaker snob market, those shoe lovers who are looking for rare and limited-edition athletic footwear. Laced Up has quickly become an authority in the booming sneaker culture.

"We carry limited editions," said Dawkins. "They might only have five hundred pairs in the whole world, and we'll carry it." An exclusive pair from Laced Up can range anywhere from $59 to $50,000. That $50,000 footwear is specifically the Nike "Sol Cal" dipped in a few champagne diamonds. The store is a favorite of several African American entertainment and political notables. But the bulk of Dawkins's customers are a diverse African American crowd who just like cool kicks.

The Designer

Celeste Johnny debuted her Johnny Vincent "See You Watching" swimwear line on BET's *Rip the Runway* in 2008 to rave reviews. The upscale swimwear line targets the cosmopolitan traveler. While several African American–owned boutiques carry her line, most of her retail clients and buyers target European women vacationing in the Caribbean. Her initial deals were with exclusive hotels in the Caribbean including Half Moon resort in Jamaica. As for her clients, they're a combination of European travelers and urban fashionistas.

The line is currently available in Barcelona, St. Vincent, Aruba, New York, Chicago, and Atlanta. The unique pieces range from $120 to $220.

The Dermatologist

Dermatologist and author Dr. Susan C. Taylor's clients wanted to know what products worked best for browner hues. So Taylor launched the skincare line RX for Brown Skin in 2007 at thirty Sephora locations. However, RX for Brown Skin doesn't solely target the African American audience. It addresses the needs of those with melanin in their skin including Latinos, Native Americans, and Asians. As of this writing, the line was available in 132 Sephora locations including a new store in Puerto Rico. It is also available in some Dillard's and Macy's stores and is especially popular in areas with large Latino populations.

LIFESTYLE LIVING

My brother Supacel creates hip-hop–inspired marketing campaigns for small businesses. Fresh out of Florida Agricultural and Mechanical University's business school, he too was inspired by the hip-hop impresario. Always one to mull over new info, he observed that the consumer increasingly dictated to the business sector.

"It's no longer about the company having a product and finding an audience or the best way to reach the audience," he said. "Businesses now have to completely retool their product at the whims and demands of the consumer. Consumers have all the power, and it's up to the business to figure them out."

I wondered how this was different from any other time in history. Isn't the customer always right?

"The speed has changed," he said. "The needs are changing faster, the consumers have no patience; plus, the consumer has more choices." No longer are typical consumers limited to the stores in their communities. If they don't like what they see, they can hop online and find competitive prices elsewhere.

Obviously the models for conventional business are getting a hefty facelift. The 2008–2009 recession, the incredible Wall Street and auto industry bailouts, and the real estate fallout, to name a few, are more than just market corrections. But in evaluating African American–owned businesses and how they traditionally operated, we can see that times have changed. While the social responsibility to the community that many black-owned businesses embraced continues, the definition of this community in light of a changing consumer base for their products changes as well.

I watched a debate once on the responsibility the business community has to create goodwill in society. One of the African American panelists spoke at length about the responsibility that corporations had to their black consumers and workforce. He discussed causes and political issues of special interest to African Americans and how corporations needed to step up and support those as well. Another panelist, a Jewish business leader, asked his contemporary why he thought corporations that were all about the bottom line and were responsible to shareholders would advocate for such special interests. "For that kind of financing," he said, "you have to look to the black business community. They would have both an affinity and the freedom to invest in such specialized causes." With changing concepts of black-owned business, I wonder how that responsibility would evolve as well.

TALENTED TENTH REVISITED
CAPITALISM VERSUS SOCIAL RESPONSIBILITY

W. E. B. Dubois's talented tenth theory continues to stir controversy in the new millennium.

I was invited to a house party a few years back. An art-loving consultant in his late thirties, Ed had purchased a spacious condominium in an old residential area that was part of the city's regentrification plans. The condo building, the lone such facility at the end of a block of older residential homes inhabited by mostly black, blue-collar retirees, stood directly across the street from a low-rise housing project. The value of Ed's condo was triple that of the average home on the block, and the few residents who lived in Ed's building were African American, postcollegiate professionals. The place was an oasis compared to the rest of the block. It was well manicured and encased in a towering, locked gate. An assortment of luxury vehicles, sport cars, and shining gas guzzlers sat within the gate's borders. Ed himself was raised in a working-class area by blue-collar parents and welcomed the opportunity to live in a neighborhood not too far from the one he grew up in. He liked the concept of a mixed-income community. But he also loved his place and the access to public transportation.

He came with no predispositions. In fact, he became active in his block club, and the flock of retirees soon championed him to become block club president. Let me note that Ed does more than his fair share of service. He's an active member of several progressive organizations and mentors young boys weekly.

Ed and one of the other condo residents decided to throw what would become an annual bash. As I pulled up the block, I could hear the buzzing of minglers half a block away. The only parking I could find was on the west side of the neighboring housing project because the typically desolate block was jammed bumper-to-bumper with high-end foreign cars. I parked accordingly and followed the cacophony of laughter up the block. As I turned the corner, I saw the divide. On one side of the street, the largely professional partygoers could be spotted through the iron gate having the time of their lives.

Laughing and dancing in a courtyard off the side of the new building, most were dressed in black with wineglasses in their hands,
music and conversation permeating the air much like the smell of
the spiced meat on the grill. But across the street stood a handful
of housing project residents who'd poured out of their homes to
see what the fuss was about. Let's just say the longtime residents
were shocked. It's one thing to know that black folks with some
financial means exist; it's another when they move across the street
from your modest, low-income apartment and throw a lavish party
you're not invited to. When I walked in, one of Ed's friends asked
me where I'd parked. I described the location, which wasn't more
than half a block away. He looked at me strangely. "Why the hell
did you park down there?" he asked, as if I'd parked on the other
side of the moon.

REFLECTIONS

When my college girlfriend Regina and I get together, after we fin-
ish updating one another on our personal lives we discuss some
tangent of the black agenda or social activism. Call it the duty of
an HBCUer, but social responsibility is as ingrained as the school
motto, the words to "Lift Every Voice and Sing," or the Pledge of
Allegiance. It doesn't help that we were both media majors, which
makes us news junkies and history buffs. Our analyses might give
those guys who solve world issues in the barbershops a run for
their money. Nevertheless, when we talk, the subjects of social
responsibility and advocacy are unavoidable.

Regina, a journalist-turned-schoolteacher reared in Chicago's
Englewood neighborhood, said that giving back was instilled in
her as a kid. "Even if I was better in a subject than my uncle, who

was my same age, or my cousin, it was my responsibility to help them improve," she said. And that drive to give back channeled her career path.

"In journalism, I felt that the minority voice was suppressed. I felt there's not a lot of diversity in the media, so that was my way of contributing to society, to offer that other voice and perspective. Teaching, for me, was a natural segue." While journalism was about educating the masses, she says, teaching is a more intimate setting in which to educate.

> I wanted to give back to the community I came up in—Englewood. I was a product of that community, and I wanted to be a role model and show kids that regardless of your circumstances, you can achieve. You don't have to use the negative experiences as a crutch. When I would come home from college I would see this hopelessness in people's faces. I didn't want to see that. I felt if there was a way to make a difference . . . The rewards in teaching are tremendous. I've had students who were gang-bangers, kids who tried to commit suicide who I talk to, I e-mail them, and they are doing well in life. I know I can't reach everyone but if I reach just twenty of them or just one, at least I know that I made an impact and helped someone stay on the right course. If I'm able to spark something in them, then they in turn can ignite something in someone else.

For many of my friends, giving back is not a choice. There is no moving up the ladder and leaving everyone behind. There is no "I get mine, you get yours" mentality. Everything from their careers to their networking to their personal service work in some way revolves around the belief that they have a mission.

It's funny, I remember attending a group discussion on giving. The mostly white assemblage of Gen X and Y yuppies was asked to share how they "gave back." Projects ranged from teaching gardening to underprivileged kids to tackling teacher positions in inner-city schools. But it was clear that the speakers were conscious of a choice in their decision to give, and most in the audience sat in awe that the speakers actually ditched the golden handcuffs to embrace their civic responsibilities. However, when the mic was passed to the two lone African American male speakers, Craig and Cory, the two brothers who'd invited me, one said that he'd grown up in a challenged neighborhood and was raised by hardworking parents who'd supported his college endeavors, and that giving back was expected. He would be a social deviant and a disappointment to his family, culture, and neighborhood if he didn't. What began as a very lighthearted affair of feel-good recitations suddenly felt heavy with my friend's obligations.

The high school dropout rates in New York City alarmed Tonya Lewis, a longtime music executive. At the time, Lewis was arranging school visits for celebrities when a lightbulb went off. "I knew we could use this to challenge students to make changes in their lives." She cofounded E.A.R.S. Entertainers 4 Education Alliance in 2004. "We utilize celebrity to reach our kids," said Lewis, who coordinates ad campaigns, PSAs, and school visits "so that those people who students look to the most are held accountable for their actions."

E.A.R.S. launched a vigorous Stay in School campaign with Hot 97, a music apprenticeship program, and the Achieve Your Dream poetry contest. It's one of many services she hopes to provide for troubled communities with her entertainment contacts. "This is a labor of love," said Lewis, an alumni of John J. College of Criminal

Justice. "The talented tenth should be the foundation of our community, but unfortunately it's not. We're not giving back. AIDS, gang warfare, these are all results of us not doing what W. E. B. DuBois said we should do."

I AM THE TALENTED TENTH

"We're the talented tenth," a colleague told me. "We're who DuBois was talking about when he wanted to create this new world."

Great, I thought, the sarcasm seeping.

"What does that mean?" I asked, knowing full well the depth of W. E. B. DuBois's historical firebomb. He reasoned in the eloquent way that would become his trademark that the top 10 percent—those African Americans privileged enough to receive higher education—was responsible for pulling up everyone else. It was expected that those with the most would help the ones with the least. Educated African Americans were to devise programs, policies, and institutions to support and uplift the masses. He advocated that only the best and the brightest go to college and predicted that all black leadership would emerge from that set. While there's nothing fundamentally wrong with it, the talented tenth concept, as with most of DuBois's assessments, can easily be misconstrued as elitism, with a self-proclaimed crew of golden few leading the masses to salvation. It echoes the white man's burden philosophy, another hats off to the notion of the well-endowed being weighted by their duty to help the helpless people of color.

The paradox in being one of the talented tenth didn't escape me. And I had the feeling that my thirtysomething colleague leaned more toward the "look, we've made it" interpretation than DuBois's take on the give-back philosophy. We, he asserted, because of our education and high-value networks, are the North Stars for the lost and trapped to follow. And the fact that we walked across the stage with diplomas in our hands, landed impressive jobs, and have some disposable income was more than most and certainly enough to count us among the "black privileged" and to make us instant leaders. I just shook my head. This can't be good. Intending social responsibility but laying the foundation for black privilege, the talented tenth concept would splinter into a duel interpretation by African Americans who continue to debate the controversial theory today.

SOCIAL RESPONSIBILITY VERSUS ELITISM

DuBois's "Talented Tenth" essay has been both hailed and maligned. Some criticize the arrogance of knighting educated blacks as societal saviors. Others take issue with limiting new black leadership to the college-educated ranks.

If there's one thing that doesn't go over well at all in the African American community, it's the thought of someone who has "made it" abandoning his or her community. There's a whole lexicon of terms and catchphrases to call out those misguided individuals. People who've achieved any modicum of success, education, or fortune become instant heroes in the black community. They're sources of pride—poster children for a strong work ethic. They're role models. But this question of success is a touchy subject, as is the concept of "making it." Education is that ladder to success, yet having an education, particularly a college-level education, is also the great divide splitting black communities today. While education has always been the gateway to opportunity, the money and opportunities hitched to the education star have rocketed beyond some people's wildest dreams. This new prospect of opportunity is pulling the rug out from under conventions.

The looming divide first becomes evident when college kids returning home suddenly find themselves out of place in their own neighborhoods. It's particularly difficult for men who find themselves worlds apart from their boyhood friends whose decisions took them elsewhere. What can make someone a source of pride can also make him an unintentional source of jealousy.

Education positions people in two very different worlds. When I give my "why you should go to college" speech to high school students, part of my argument is that they won't even know this new world of opportunity exists without the exposure. I feel a person can make wonderful contributions without a diploma on his or her wall, but lack of access to other social stratospheres hems in many people. Even those with goo gobs of cash, short of some claim to fame or celebrity, experience a definitive social barricade. The divide is mind-boggling. Blacks who have graduated from college and those who haven't socialize in two very different worlds. They don't go to the same events. They don't go to the same parties, the same grocery stores, the same malls. They don't join the same networking groups. Unintentionally, friends can wind up on two very different paths and living two very different lifestyles, sometimes advocating for opposing interests.

I gave this some thought when I began working with a mentor program. The coordinator mentioned that the kids didn't often see "people like you." It took me a moment to come out of my bubble and figure out who people like me were. When I did, I then wondered how that was possible with the number of volunteer groups rising and with people like me living everywhere. It hit me that it was a dire problem if the only time many young black kids in the city saw people like me was at a well-intentioned but underfunded community group meeting. It reminded me of the tensions between college students and the residents of the housing projects that surrounded the Atlanta University Center (AUC) in the 1990s. Spike Lee made reference to this conflict in his cult classic *School Daze*. Students were having growing conflicts with the "locals."

At the AUC, a Caribbean-born professor discussed ways to end the friction, suggesting that more of us volunteer with neighborhood community programs. "Maybe that's the problem," I said. "If the only time we interact is when we're mentoring or doling out advice, doesn't that make it seem as if we think we're fundamentally better than them? Maybe we should have parties or events together or encourage dating or something." "Parties? Dating? Absolutely not," he said. Two parallel worlds. Two different experiences.

I mentioned this to Craig, a friend of mine who charged that I was being elitist when I told him that based on his education and lifestyle, and mine as well, 75 percent of the people he talked to were probably college graduates, which facilitated a divide whether we were conscious of it or not. He argued that he made great efforts to be friendly to everyone and didn't speak to people or not on the basis of their education. Well, who does? I wondered. Oh, yeah, the elite. "OK," I said. "List the ten people you talk to the most in a given week, not including family. How many of them went to college?" It came to eight out of ten. The ninth person was his mother, whom he insisted on including, and the tenth was a guy who studied in a nontraditional path. Craig got my point, but he wasn't happy about it. He was an active mentor and volunteer. "So that's supposed to make me elitist?" he retorted. "Who said anything about elitism?" I asked. You see, no socially conscious African American person wants to buy into the intra-ethnic us-versus-them debate. And they certainly don't want to be pegged as elitist.

Not everyone who falls into the talented tenth category has divorced him- or herself from the community, but not everyone is readily digging in to do work, either. While service is held high and talked about proudly, with many young African Americans working diligently to make a difference, the capitalist reins on our society more often than not tug on the interests of those most readily able to take advantage of it. Their inner turmoil is evident.

THE DEBATE

"I think the whole concept of the talented tenth has been misconstrued as a thing about class," said author Kenji Jasper. "It's a thing about ability. Those of us who are gifted enough or enabled enough to get beyond the obstacles that prevent too many of us from going to college should get together to help everyone as a whole." The Morehouse alum frequently works with youth organizations and speaks at schools.

Higher education is not a requisite for helping anyone.

"All goodwill is not based on academic achievement," said Jody Brockington, former director of alumni affairs for National Urban Fellows, Inc., an organization that grooms people of color for graduate degrees in public administration, a program Brockington participated in as a student.

If higher achievement, DuBois's primary requisite for talented tenth action, isn't pertinent, is the theory still relevant?

"I think the talented tenth theory is very relevant," Cory Stevenson shared. A graduate of the University of Minnesota, he mentors boys, leads art workshops for kids, and conducts voter registration drives annually. "Access to education isn't equal. So those who get a quality education have to give back or show others how to obtain an education. I think it's practical; I just don't think it's put into practice."

What DuBois did not expect and addressed many years later was that some in the talented tenth ranks would embrace their hard-fought higher education to forge a greater divide between themselves and those who needed their skills the most.

"What he didn't anticipate was that once they got the success they would do the same thing as everyone else," said Hal Smith, a community educator and research consultant whose clients include youth organizations and outreach groups. A Harvard graduate and former professor, Smith has witnessed debates among his peers and cringed at the sense of entitlement accrued by rising black professionals.

"These people didn't become educated and become more service oriented but were much more invested in themselves. It became the ultimate extension of all the things we were struggling against.

"You've achieved a certain amount, and you owe that service back, but it leads to elitism. People start to feel that they got their membership in the talented tenth by themselves only and don't appreciate the sacrifices people made to get there and to be there."

REGENTRIFICATION: THE CAPITALIST DIVIDE

Michelle moved into Bronzeville with all the enthusiasm of a kindergartner starting school. Bronzeville, a historic black Chicago neighborhood with longtime residents, had fallen on hard times in recent decades, but with a healthy dose of interest from banks and real estate agents, the area became hot property in the 2K. It would be the new home for countless black professionals eager to stay in the communities they'd sprung from. Michelle moved across the street from Washington Park, "the Central Park of the South Side," she chimed proudly. Businesses would open up, she said. Schools would be revitalized, and newcomers, people like herself, would move in en masse. The neighborhood was changing, and she was thrilled with the prospect of her rising property values. She hosted an array of affairs at her home and began investing in other properties in the area, waiting for that moment of change. Michelle was an active participant in several professional organizations of young African Americans and was a big proponent of networking and supporting black businesses. The promise was rooted in reality. Small businesses did trickle in, and young professionals began acquiring area properties in droves. With talk of the Olympic Games coming to town and plans for a stadium to be built in her neighborhood park, Michelle had dancing dollar signs in her head. Now it was just a waiting game. To her credit, her enthusiasm didn't wane quickly but was chipped away by a series of incidents that made her feel unwelcome. First people began stealing things off her back porch. Then her car was broken into. Then it was broken into several more times. She figured it must be inhabitants of an area goodwill center that provided food and clothing to homeless drug addicts. While typically she'd be an advocate of such a center and its services, she soon wished the center would shut its doors. But it, too, would soon disappear, she figured, along with various "nuisance" factors that inhabited the park she liked walking her dogs in.

But longtime residents, concerned about rising property taxes and a systematic plan to push them out of their neighborhood, began protesting the Olympic Games. Nearby housing projects had already been demolished, and hundreds of residents were given vouchers to live elsewhere. As a result, several community schools had shut down, and the dream that would give Michelle increased dollar value became a nightmare for longtime residents, who saw access to their own community coming to a dramatic end. These longtime residents didn't want the Games in their city, didn't want a stadium in their neighborhood, and didn't want higher taxes to push them out of the communities they loved.

As community tensions grew, Michelle's place was robbed. Concerned about safety, she moved into a neighboring property, a spacious home she had remodeled to her liking. But her construction workers were robbed, too. Someone broke out her back windows. Her garage was vandalized. She had a few Peeping Tom incidents. She flirted with moving. Then the housing market tanked, and the value of her home no longer matched her investment. The neighborhood, she complains, still doesn't have a real shopping mall or a fully functional grocery store. The promise of community reinvestment has fallen short. For all the taxes we pay in this area we deserve more, she argues. She's also angry with the mostly white suburban protectors who routinely come into her neighborhood to protest the Games and defend the working-class residents. "Tell them to go march in their own neighborhoods," she said. "I want the Olympics to come because I want my property values to rise and for the quality of life to change around here."

"What about the hardworking people in the area who can't afford the taxes?" I asked. They're targets of crime, too. But Michelle doesn't have much to say about them. On the other hand, she does have a growing list of friends and associates with similar horror stories. All of them are waiting for their neighbors to be priced out.

I GOT MINE, YOU GET YOURS

"[Many people] turn our backs on the less fortunate," said Alton Tinker, former president of the National Black MBA Association of

Cleveland and founder of the Society of Young Professionals. "We figure if we did it, they should do it, too." While Tinker claims he doesn't agree, it is a rampant belief among his associates, he said.

"It's like you've made it and you are the model," said Hal Smith of those who devalue service. "They seem to think that if they could get everyone to act like them, their work is done. It's too finished. It's as if they don't need to do anything other than have people model their achievement."

The bootstrap theory is alive and well. Criticism by upper- and middle-class African Americans of their working-class brethren is common. The assumption is if we did it, they should be able to, with little thought given to the social factors and institutions that create their situation, said Smith.

Smith credits this disconnect between the classes to a lack of relationship to the larger community and a break in the sense of legacy.

"A lot of folks who do feel that way, who are very much invested in elitism, who see it as power *over* and not power *with*, they are people who don't understand our struggle," said Smith.

A lack of intergenerational and interclass communication impedes progress as well.

"We're afraid of one another," said Tinker, pointing to the media's exaggeration of crime among blacks. "The media plays into how we think. I'm scared to say something if I see a group of guys hanging on the corner."

Tinker says he tried to overcome his fears. He volunteers with schools and frequently speaks to schoolchildren. But even he was surprised at his initial reactions when he was assigned to mentor a troubled twelve-year-old boy he'd met through friends at a ski club. "Initially, I didn't think we would gel. He was a tough-looking kid, and I formed an opinion that didn't have any basis. But as I talked to him, I realized I was incorrect." They developed a healthy relationship. The boy now attends college on the East Coast, a decision Tinker knows he helped facilitate.

SERVICE OR NETWORKING?

According to the U.S. Census Bureau, in 2004 approximately 17 percent (up from 12 percent a decade earlier) of African Americans held bachelor's degrees, compared to 30 percent of whites. In DuBois's day, the number was well under 3 percent. Yet the history of African American–based philanthropy and charity predates the Civil War. Many organizations with roots in service, black sororities and fraternities, NAACP, Rainbow PUSH, the Southern Christian Leadership Conference (SCLC), the Student Nonviolent Coordinating Committee (SNCC), the Urban League, and a host of others do, in fact, emerge from the college-educated ranks.

Today thousands of charitable organizations, political activist groups, and an array of other groups address issues from health care to poverty. An increasing number of black professional groups with service arms have emerged, too: 100 Black Men, the Urban League's Metropolitan Board and Young Professionals Board, the National Black MBA Association—each with chapters in multiple cities. And the list continues.

But even as these organizations swell, the question about the commitment of black professionals to service remains, with some charging that the majority of African American professional and service-based groups are thinly veiled networking sessions and largely self-serving.

"[To many,] professional organizations are mostly feel goods," said Dale Jackson, a director with the Service Employees International Union (SEIU) in Chicago. Jackson works with several political organizations as well. "There are measurable differences that they are doing. Members get to say, 'I'm a part of this organization.' I'm not saying you shouldn't do that, but collectively what happens?"

Oddly, service work is a new-wave networking tool. Participation on service-oriented boards boosts résumés; donating to the charity of the month can be "cool." Attending a fashionably swank party in which a small percentage of the proceeds goes to a worthy cause can be identified as giving back. But is it?

Jackson compares organizing to pulling teeth when he taps his peers for hands-on service work. "There's a core group of people who give back," he said. "The others may give you a hundred dollars for a ticket or donate a can of soup, but they're not getting up at 7:00 A.M. to put the work in."

It's the work in the field that is often neglected. "What's missing on greater levels are relationships and time. Donating money is always appreciated. Most organizations I've worked with are criminally underfunded," said Smith. "You can write your check for a thousand dollars, and the organization would love it. But what if you could give fifty hours a year?"

Jody Brockington, who also sits on the board of the literacy program Behind the Book, has dedicated her life to service. "I've worked in the nonprofit sector my whole career," she said. "What they would consider to be the black Ivy groups and those of us who achieved, I think, are giving our fair share, but I think there's some confusion." Brockington also served as director of corporate relations and fund development at the New York Urban League and as president of their Young Professionals Board. "I think there are so many ways to assist that people feel overwhelmed. If you want to mentor and help a kid today there are fifty thousand programs.

I can go to a fundraiser every day if I wanted. I can go to an Alvin Ailey event, then the MBA conference, the MLK luncheon."

"We feel that the work ahead is too big and too amorphous," said Smith. "It was clear what we needed to do in the 1960s, instead of understanding that those were just benchmarks in a longer, more complex fight. We don't feel that it's connected to what's going on right now."

But another take is that societal change seems so overwhelming. Focusing on the microcosm—your personal life, your family—can be a full-time job in and of itself. But those who prioritize service say that's not an excuse.

"If I took the position that I'm just going to focus on me and my family, I still have to be concerned with other people who have not given their children those same morals and values," my friend Regina says. "So I never get to the point where I feel I can be removed from the situation. If someone is in need, you can't ever be removed from it. It's not 'them and me.' We all see that with the economy. When the economy is messed up and inflation goes up, crime escalates. It doesn't just impact those in the inner city. We're all connected. Until people understand that, we will continue to face these issues. I don't think you can ever reach a level of complacency. There is always a way you can contribute."

NEOFEMINISM
WOMANIST VALUES IN THE AGE OF THE VIDEO GIRL

*New opportunities
for women redefine female
identity in the new age.*

A group of people I affectionately call the Crew goes out to dinner periodically. There are six of us, four men and two women, and we were gummed together because we found ourselves the unlikely superheroes in an organization whose leadership was nosediving it into chaos. But the Crew, when not dissecting leadership or solving the world calamity of the day, usually pitched verbal pennies on relationship matters into the conversation pool. As the dialogue snaked from one battle of the wits to the next, one subject the guys all seemed to agree on was that I and the other woman in the Crew were "man women." It was a term of endearment, they argued. Not that they questioned our heterosexuality. Nor were they inferring we were zealot fembots or antimale. They just felt that our lovely, feminine exteriors were a bit deceiving, some new-age cloak for a very male way of thinking we embodied that they, as men, were both intrigued and perplexed by at the same time. Our male-to-female thinking ratio was 55 percent guy, 45 percent woman. I don't know how they came up with those numbers. I didn't know what they were talking about.

"You just don't think like other women," they reasoned.

"And how do other women think?" I asked. Digging for words, these verbal wizards were rendered speechless.

I bumped into this notion a few times, with another guy friend sharing the same thing. "You just have this guy thing. You enjoy competing with men." Of course I disagreed. After some amusing verbal somersaults on the subject he asked me to name one distinctly feminine activity I participated in.

"What's a distinctly feminine activity? Like picking flowers?"

"Picking flowers?" he said. "Who does that?"

"Having a period? Getting my hair done?"

"No. I'm not talking about health and grooming. I'm not talking about the way you dress. I'm talking about activities that are associated with women that men aren't interested in."

It was an interesting notion, so I flipped through my mental Rolodex of activities. I've worked in film and in journalism, and film, more so than journalism, was certainly male dominated behind the scenes. Most of my business partners were men. When I was writing like a madwoman, I'd taken to running, and I was in a serious running-through-the-snow phase. Was that masculine? I wondered. Then there's my weekly all-male kung fu class. I did some of the workouts on Exercise TV; surely that could go in the feminine box. Dance class? Was that feminine? I was a few seconds shy of counting my women friends when I figured maybe there's something to this.

However, as I tallied up my traditional male versus traditional female activities, my greatest problem was figuring out the difference. I was taught at birth that I could be anything from astronaut to beauty queen, so the notion of an activity being feminine or masculine totally eluded me. Men and women could do just about the same things. Women could exemplify physical prowess in sports, run businesses, and lead organizations and families. Where we weren't dominant, we were at least present, and outside of our anatomical differences it never dawned on me there was such a thing as a male activity.

What's a male activity? Hammering stuff? Chucking down shots at Super Bowl parties? Shoveling snow?

In fact, I'd probably gone out of my way to demonstrate in small ways that there was no such thing as a man thing. When my younger brother was blessed with action figures and wrestling dolls, I played with them, too. When rap was first hitting radio, my brother and I decided to battle one another. It never happened, but my aim was to show that I could do it, too. I even got a kick out of testing my dad. When he'd remind me that he'd "support me in anything" as a kid, I'd kick back all kinds of traditionally male gigs I could hypothetically have and ask, precociously, if he'd support me.

"Hey, Dad. What if I wanted to be a professional body builder? Would you support me in that?"

"Absolutely."

"What if I wanted to be a wrestler?"

"I'd support you in that, too," he said, raising an eyebrow. I tried to think of a really good one.

"What if I wanted to be a professional football player?"

"Why would you want to do that?"

And for a hot minute, I did think it would be cool if I could play football. I'd read about a couple of girls in a high school league, and while I couldn't envision my small frame surviving a tackle pileup, I did enjoy knowing that if I tried, I could. I could at least throw a football, right? Surely by the time I became an adult, there would be a professional women's football league. Why not? But growing up I was anything but a tomboy. I was a studious, somewhat quiet, well-mannered girl who did her homework, took dance classes, and had a kick-butt rock collection. But I refused to like pink, because girls were *supposed* to like pink. Nor was I big on teen fashion rags plastered with faces of older-looking women I certainly didn't resemble giving me advice on how to call a boy and alleviate pimples. On the other hand, I was captain of my pom-pom squad, a traditional move for women in athletics. And pom-pom, let me remind you, is a sport, too.

So after a flash flood of thoughts on the matter, I returned to my friend and responded.

"I don't even know what a woman's activity is. Give me an example."

"That's my point," he said laughing. "It's all good, that's just you."

■ ■ ■

Women pushing the boundaries of sex roles is nothing new. Harriet Tubman wielded a gun and led slaves through hell and high water to freedom; Shirley Chisholm ran for president. And there's a rich history of black women taking charge, sometimes out of necessity, other times by choice.

The past decade has been all about the superhero phenomenon of "you're a free woman; you can do it all." In today's world, where you have Michelle Obama, Beyoncé, and Serena Williams making headlines, there's no question that a black woman can both wear nail polish and fix a tire. She can get her hair styled and run track. She can lead a team of men and still write poetry. Have a family and a career. She can take a stripper aerobics class and be president of the PTA. It's not like never the two shall meet.

Many women today experiment with everything. Changing careers like wigs, going through men like water, and following every fancy our hearts desire. A few years back I wrote a story on a phenomenon called the twentysomething crisis, a bout of conflict akin to a midlife crisis but which was hitting a younger set—those in their twenties and thirties who felt all was lost if they hadn't secured the house, the car, the man, the kids, the comfy job, the rising 401K, a fist-sized Chihuahua, and a shout-out in a rap song by age thirty. I spoke to countless young, ambitious women, some who were doing serious juggling: hopscotching among school, two part-time jobs, a child, and a pogo stick of a relationship while simultaneously launching their nonprofit and first entrepreneurial venture.

Doing it all became the new-age path to success, and with the multihyphenate now in vogue, women who already had a tendency to take on other people's problems were now fighting depression over the difficulty in having it all. Whereas having it all used to mean finding work and family balance, now it meant literally having it *all*. It's what our predecessors fought for. It's called choice. But with this fanfare of freedom comes the empty nostalgia for a yesteryear that probably never really existed. A yesteryear of safety and security when men provided for women, when going for that golden corner office didn't mean a life wrestling with change, when the pressures of having it all weren't so debilitating. Stories of female corporate executives "opting out" to be housewives— news blasts on women who didn't want to rope-climb the career ladder—filtered through the media. I dismissed it as largely over-hyped hogwash until I led a workshop with a group of African American college-bound teens. When the students took turns sharing their career aspirations, one bright girl revealed that she wanted to be a housewife.

"How are you going to make money?"

"My husband will do all that. I'm just going to college to find a husband."

After checking my Blackberry calendar to make sure it was in fact the new millennium, I considered detailing the virtue of being self-sufficient or debating the probability of her finding a relationship in which income and money wouldn't be an issue. I could have told horror stories of women left high and dry by husbands and forced to make it on their own. On the other hand, she very well could find a well-to-do husband and live a happy life as a homemaker. I don't know if you should set goals for that lot in life, but in an age when you can be anything, should I muffle her *Better Homes and Gardens* dream? Even engaging in a debate felt ridiculous. I figured a few years in college would open her eyes to other choices. The girl could just be bewitched by too many seasons of

Desperate Housewives. Who knows? But the fact remained that a seventeen-year-old, college-bound student felt perfectly comfortable announcing to a class of her peers in this day and age that she hoped to be a housewife.

I personally wasn't intrigued by this fairy-tale nostalgia, but many women flirted with it. "Finding good men" and "being sexy" felt like code words for the same old traditional endeavors for women being packaged in the guise of self-empowerment.

I think today some reflection has brought women back to the pressing question they must ask themselves: *What do you want to do?* Or, echoing the oracle in *The Matrix*, *What's your purpose?*

It's this new focus on a purpose-centered life, in which our goals aren't just about proving ourselves to the world or to men, that is causing a reassessment of everything.

AGE OF BONDAGE

I have a problem with women's events. It's not something I'm particularly proud of, and it smells of an erudite twist on women hating women. But I don't think that's what this is.

I've just found that I have a fundamental disinterest in some of the more traditional women's cohesiveness activities popping up. Not that I have a problem bonding with or networking with women. In fact, there's a serious need to boost the network capacity among women of all colors. But there is something to the way we've coalesced around this identity as women that is amorphous.

Bound by duty, I've attended the women's conferences with the health workshops, career-building seminars, financial-empowerment workshops, and relationship forums. A healthy dose of advice always floats around; attendees look happy, and we carry our pink goodie bags filled with promotional lipsticks and chamomile-scented soaps.

But I always feel claustrophobic at these affairs. There's just got to be more to womanhood than finding a husband, having great sex, displaying the fashion flair of the week, and finding a career that makes you self-sufficient and happy.

Gloria Steinem said that women should be the husbands they want to marry. Live life on your terms, create the life you want, reach for the stars. But while many women at these gatherings have one foot firmly planted in the promise of the future, the other is cemented in the virtues of the past. A hybrid of *Sex and the City*, *Working Girl*, and *Moulin Rouge*.

But it is the sense of need that feels the most overwhelming.

In many of these blossoming groups and events I feel like we're wearing masks, dancing around a cauldron of pain—a brew of relationship drama, insecurity issues, work battles, and lovelessness we drink to bind us together like sticks of dynamite. The main ingredient in our brew is men. Men are at the heart of every issue, and I feel like we are "keep ya head up" soldiers marching toward triumph to circumvent the next heartbreak in search of "the one." I'm not saying these breakout moments aren't important, I just don't get why so many events for women always boil down to a heart-to-heart talk about men. Can we blame men for everything? Everything?

The collective definition of a woman seems—how can I say this?—dated.

Is womanhood just a code word for "victim" with "men suck" as the subtext? While women experience any range of tragic and not-so-tragic hurts throughout their lives, to embrace victimhood as if it were organic to our sex feels like a self-deprecating belief that fosters self-sabotage. It's like we're self-proclaimed martyrs, always trying to overcome something, always trying to "be strong" or "sacrifice for the team." But very little emphasis is placed on being ourselves.

The flip side to embracing martyrdom is the sunny-side-up approach to womanhood in which an array of beauty aids and spa services are packaged as the magic solution to our problems and the key to uncovering our femininity. A scented candle in the bathtub, holistic spa retreats, group manicures, waxing parties. These things, according to articles and blogs, are our bonding agents, and while no one should have to turn down a good massage, I just feel, goodness, there's got to be another way.

So if we aren't discussing the man problem of the month or shelling out dough for monthly bikini waxing, what the heck would we be talking about?

Something is missing from this dialogue.

VIDEO GIRL DREAMS

I've grown weary of talking about the video girl. Yeah, I've seen her. She's been shake-dancing on my TV screen for nearly two decades now. She's a caramel-to-brown woman with waist-long locks and curls and perfect lips and hips gyrating to the hottest beat of the week. She's the silent arm-piece in songs in which the testosterone is as heavy as the bass. She's a vixen, a vamp. Year by year her sex-laced ways, her looks and likes, keep upping the ante of achievability.

But I like her. I like her because she's single-handedly brought curves and the beauty of browner women to the mainstream, giving those model-thin images a Flo Jo run for their money. She's probably sent more black women to the gym than Thanksgiving dinner. But few want to hear about that side. When I mentioned it to an editor who asked me to write on vixens and sexism, she said snappily, "Well, we're not focusing on that." End of subject.

The video vixen is not as mighty as Wonder Woman. She doesn't have the guts of Pam Grier's Foxy Brown. In fact, she doesn't really speak, just slithers like a snake from one side of the screen to the other.

Yes, she's oversexed. Sometimes she's faceless. She does have a serious propensity for stirring insecurities. She tends to be on one end of the color spectrum more than the other. She's never bigger than a size 5. She's not really happy or sad, just ready-made for action. But she wears cool stuff—death-defying stilettos, bust-squeezing halters. And if you can catch a glimpse of her face, you can pick up a makeup tip or two. I've decided to befriend rather than make an enemy out of her because there's no point in blaming Video Vixen for our problems, either.

I'm not trying to make light of the sexualization of black women or all women in our nation's treasured past. Nor do I deny she can have an impact on your self-esteem if you soak in her gaze too long. A half hour of video watching on a bad day could send your heart south.

But I'd be remiss if I didn't note that the video girl is not real. Her one-sided image isn't even of her own making.

Sure, the women playing her are real. Models or around-the-way girls with Coca Cola–bottle shapes crammed into a few seconds of eye-candy pleasure, some have hustled their way to calendar pinup status. But I don't care if she has had plastic surgery, if she wears a weave, or if she's chiseled her shape body-slamming into trees all day. And the blogging frenzy over who's had what surgery, who didn't have surgery, and who's dating whom could be a national pastime. I just don't partake.

She's just not that important.

I think there's something to be said about us as women viewers when we buy wholesale into images that aren't real and then take them so seriously.

If it's that doggone offensive, turn it off.

I used to think that the video girl's vilification resulted from having fewer images of black women onscreen in general. Outside of a handful of actresses, reporters, Condoleezza Rice, and now Ms. Obama, the numbers were slim. But then I remembered another hallmark in pop culture lore that no one was factoring into the video girl debate: Oprah. Oprah, the first black woman billionaire, queen of media and an inspiration to millions, is a nontraditional image if there ever was one. Oprah is nearly omnipresent. On TV daily, on satellite radio, in movies, running and appearing in magazines, she has been a media force for more than twenty-five years. She is more famous than all of the nameless vixens combined. She's powerful, smart, relatable, and attractive, but even she, for some strange reason, hasn't tipped the image scale enough to keep video vixens from being panned on panels and women's conferences all over.

Then I thought about images of white women in the media. The numbers are larger, the images more diverse. But Barbara Bush, Martha Stewart, and Hillary Clinton combined can't trump the media's infatuation with a sultry Britney Spears video.

So on some level, black women are choosing to elevate the video girl's image into notoriety despite images of more powerful women on the screen.

But why?

I don't know what it is about Americans and fantasy, where we've got to see it in pictures. As African Americans we've justifiably been sensitive to our image because it's one thing we never controlled.

But in a mass-media world where image is now fantasy and what's real doesn't make Nielson ratings, why look to the image for an understanding of reality at all?

Pop culture has largely been a kaleidoscope of our heightened fantasies and wants, dreams and wishes, desires and lust. It tugs at our emotions; it draws us to the screen. While the business behind it and the players are real, are we looking for the video girl to do things that she's simply not made to do?

I think the biggest beef we have with the video girl is wirelessly connected to our own dirty little secret: we want to be her. Not forever, mind you. Not even for a full day. How many of us can sit propped up on a jagged rock in a thong bikini with an alluring smile on our face? Nor do we want to look exactly like her. But for a brief moment we want to be enticing and sexy and have someone think we're drop-dead desirable, too.

It's this sexuality piece that feminists can't seem to fully integrate into our ideology. Women want to work the same jobs as men, we want equal pay, we want day care, we want safe families, and we don't want to be violated and harassed. We want to have the freedom to date whom we please, marry if we want, and not be berated for expressing our sexuality. But at the same time, women want to be desired, too. That murky water of desire drops us smack-dab into the middle of sexist images 101. Sexy doesn't have to mean impossible shoes and breathless corsets, but sometimes it does. Truth is, you can be sexy in a mildewed potato sack if you work it right. But what about those, and obviously the numbers skyrocket into the millions of people, whose image of sexy mimics the video girl we're all taught to hate? Are we being force-fed images of what sexy is or are we dictating those images by playing into the fantasy?

PROPAGANDA GAMES

A couple years back, a guy who shall remain nameless got the black, female Internet users of the world dragon-fire hot when he announced his plans to launch a gentleman's club for black men. Men had to pay some astronomical amount to join, whereas the women didn't need to pay anything, just fit the age and size requirements. Black women became livid. It didn't help when this guy got on the radio and said, in short, if you don't look like Halle Berry, don't come knocking. Callers were incensed. But that's not all. He then went into a laundry list of the problems with black women and why the club would be so strict about which ladies qualified. We were either crazed workaholics looking for men, crazed workaholics who didn't need men, despots who couldn't get men, or gold diggers snatching up rich men whenever possible. So the screening process would be tight. The phones were ringing off the hook. Women with emotion-riddled voices tried to argue him down. While his logic was flawed, his laser-sharp focus was tight, and none of them could out-argue him without getting lost in their own storm. This guy somehow finagled his way into being the guest speaker at a women's expo. That's right, a women's expo. And women drove for miles to tell him off.

I wasn't there, but someone told me about it. Hundreds of women booed and hissed. They snapped on him. They called him every name in the book. The guy sat there with a smug grin. He'd won.

My question: Why?

Not "Why were they mad?" This guy's logic was beyond offensive; it was totally idiotic and fanned the flames of the "who is beautiful and who is not" mentality that we all hoped was dead and buried. And not "Why was he chosen to speak?" Obviously his knack for controversy was the draw. But rather "Why would women pay hard-earned cash out of their own pockets for an event, costly parking, and overpriced food to ceremonially curse out an idiot whose speaker fee we were paying for?"

I think we let our emotions get the best of us.

I read once that you should never let people know when you're angry, because once they know your trigger, they'll use it for their own purposes. Not that every guy is walking around with a remote control with a flip-her-wig button, but it served as a reminder not to let everything set us off. Women are judged to be emotional. Black women especially are stereotyped that way.

I just wonder if how we define ourselves as women is reactionary. When we discuss femininity, are we just scratching the surface with products and services? They're an aspect of who we are but just that, one aspect, to be balanced with our masculine side as well.

Returning to the Crew, I asked one of the guys to give me some clarity on this "man woman" description. "You're a man woman because you have masculine drive. Because you like freedom and nonattachment," he said.

Freedom, drive, and nonattachment were the cornerstones of the traits our feminist foremothers wanted us to have.

In this age of authenticity, and with the sheer will we have to fine-tune in a world that tells us that being ourselves isn't enough, to be feminine or just female is a double-edged sword.

Emotions, balanced or not, don't seem to have a place in a world where ambition is king. We embrace femininity as a feel-good tool, not the key to our own empowerment, and the result is a bit of internal conflict. Can a woman be herself and, say, run a business? Can a woman be fully aware of her emotions and win an argument? Or do we always feel we have to wield our masculine sides, placing our emotions, sexuality, and affinity for pretty things in a neat box to effectively compete? Why do I buckle to the pressure to compete with men when no one can out-compete me in being me?

As a kid I sensed that doing "girly things"—rocking baby dolls, baking in the Easy-Bake oven—weren't respected in the way that tackling some poor kid on the football field was. Was my own definition of womanhood reactionary, too?

The more women focus on self-expression, the more empowered we'll be. There's a power in breaking the mold but also a power in discovering ourselves beyond the chokeholds of feminine and masculine definitions.

Once again, this contemplation takes us right back to square one: ourselves.

10

THE OBAMA FACTOR
REDEFINING POSSIBILITY

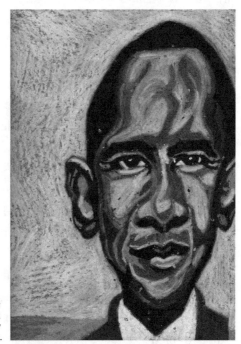

President Barack Obama is changing the paradigm of leadership and possibility in America.

It was the weekend before Tuesday's general election. Riding shotgun in a Chrysler 300, I flipped through a list of registered voters in
Indianapolis public housing. My mom, an official Obama volunteer,
was taking her fourth trip to Indiana, our neighboring red state—a
state that had voted Republican in the presidential election for the
past thirty years but with Obama fever now had a serious blue
leaning. Because of Indiana's close proximity to Illinois, its closing
factories prompting many to rethink their Republican loyalties, its
half million new voters, and its impressive get-out-the-vote efforts
in Northwest Indiana, the Obama campaign was asking Chicago-
area volunteers to hit I-80 and seal the deal.

That same weekend, my younger sister, Veronica, was boasting
on how she was hopping medians in Herndon, Virginia, with some
friends, posting Obama signs along the road. While a great deal of
my work was some spirited blogging, I figured it was time to step
away from Internet politics and do some fieldwork. My mom, who
in her free time was either working local Obama phone banks, mail-
ing Obama postcards, or buying the latest Obama paraphernalia,
had become a de facto campaign rep for friends, family, and associates and had recruited me. With a car chock-full of foil-wrapped
turkey sandwiches, fruit, and Obama stickers, my mom and I pulled
up to our destination. Clad in all black and leather jackets, we
looked like smiling new-age Panthers and total outsiders, which
is why we were spotted among the flock of sunny Midwest volunteers who flooded the Indianapolis headquarters and asked to
canvass the city's housing projects. So out door-hopping we went.
Frankly, the all-black residents were shocked to see us, and smiles
crept across their lips as it became evident that this campaign did
not take their vote for granted. Some residents needed rides to the
polls; most needed clarity on early voting locations and poll sites.
Others wanted assurance that their vote would count. And the fever

spread. Newly registered teens wanted to rock the stickers I gave them on their hoodies, single moms wanted stickers for their toddlers' Tonka trucks. A few wanted to post 'em smack-dab on their apartment door.

It was one of those rare moments I knew I should crystallize for my kids' and grandkids' sake. While my parents could tell winding tales about their memories of King's "I Have a Dream" speech, 1960s campus protests, or a spirit-raising election or two, my greatest "where were you" moments had to do with hip-hop songs, 9/11, and a Sox championship.

Professor Michael Eric Dyson talks about something called cultural amnesia, illustrating that the so-called hip-hop generation has turned, in absence of massive protests or epic civil rights battles, to pop culture for its civic barometer. It's a default mechanism. We have no common memories of socially important events and causes that don't just symbolically reenact the achievements of previous generations, so instead we are infused with a love affair for pop culture and armchair news analysis. Gen Xers may not have clear memories of where they were when the Berlin Wall fell, when the Gulf War under Bush the First began, or when welfare was dismantled, but we do remember our inaugural listen to Diddy's "All About the Benjamins" (college weekend in Cancun), when Tupac was murdered (Atlanta, senior year, Clark Atlanta University), and where we heard that *Honey* magazine, a mag for black women hipsters, closed its doors (NYC, Tao Restaurant).

On the other hand, I don't remember when I first used the defining technological devices of the past decade, and I doubt they rank as even fuzzy memories for my peers, either. My aunt had fond stories fit for fireside chats about when she first saw color television. When did I first use the Internet? When did I send my first text message? Buy my first Blackberry? I don't have a clue.

This isn't to make light of my generation and the challenges of the postmodern world, our politics or empathies, but it is to say that the scope of our idealism was chain-locked to our moneymaking aspirations or the candid inspiration from a Top 40 hit. Few if any of us expected our politicians to be more than self-serving hams who sold out their constituencies on the regular. But our jaded outrage was limited to heated conversations at house parties, in chat rooms, and on cell phones. Some of us took jobs and adopted personal missions to empower the unempowered. Others crammed their days with an assortment of volunteer and civic activities. However, we relegated our idealistic nostalgia to symbolic gestures: rocking a peace sign on a pair of jeans, wearing an Afro for old times' sake, donating canned goods and coats on Christmas, or reading Oprah's book of the month.

At best we volunteered, voted, went green, or put our dollars behind the latest worthy cause. But even we knew this wasn't enough.

So Obama's candidacy was the first major grassroots political effort that most Gen Xers and Yers could participate in that resonated on the national level with anything remotely reminiscent of the civil rights movements of the past. Sure, some of us were a part of the Free South Africa efforts and others walked in the Million Man March, Jena 6 protests, Sudan crisis-awareness campaigns, or antiwar demonstrations. We gave money and clothes to Katrina victims and to the tsunami victims in the Pacific, but for the most part there was no national cause to rekindle the idealism of my peers, certainly not one that received mainstream coverage, and no proverbial lightning rod to get it started.

So where was I minutes before Obama was predicted to win the election? I, in a nervous effort to stay calm in case the inevitable did not happen, was racing up the Dan Ryan Expressway to my mom's Obama party downtown, trying to dodge Millennium Park traffic in the Chi while stressing how I was going to attend the other five Obama celebration parties I was invited to and still get back south to pick up a friend who wanted to tag along. I was also firmly focused on thinking about anything but the possibility of a McCain win.

It was oddly warm, nearly seventy degrees on what would typically be a snowy day. With visions of the never-ending 2000 election in my head, in which the final count was several days late and stymied with a politically tinged Supreme Court decision, I figured I wouldn't know a winner until at least 2:00 A.M., enough time to zigzag through the city and avoid the *What if?* mind chatter of an Obama loss. Which, with all the hype and sheer revelry, I simply couldn't entertain.

But electricity sent shock waves through the air. Those afraid to show too much enthusiasm began to etch away at the facade of pessimism, and others were gestating bundles of glee waiting for a victory they'd already claimed. I hopped out of the car, sashayed through the winding lobby and up the elevator prepared for a never-ending night. However, by the time I walked the hallway to my mom's suite I could hear the beaming cheers. Perhaps Obama had won a swing state—Indiana, hopefully—or maybe someone had told a really funny joke. So when I opened the door and saw the CNN news flash predicting Obama the winner, my eyeballs were glued to the screen. Someone hurriedly shoved a plastic champagne flute in my hand. With the exception of my mom, who was flitting about like Tinkerbell, the rest of us partyers were Old Testament pillars of salt, stunned by the magnitude of hope realized.

I think we glowed.

It felt like the planet shifted. It was a fundamental mental flip; a stratospheric ceiling was busted, old mind-sets stomped to smithereens. Hope—the North Star for dreamers mired in the muck of reality—had finally made good on the promise.

Obama won, and he won definitively.

Had I ever stood witness to change of this magnitude? Had I ever seen national hope resurrected?

I don't think so.

For weeks leading up to the election, the nervous possibility of America's first African American president became the cooling mist in the political fire. Trepidatious pragmatists became jittery believers, longtime supporters waved Barack banners like cheerleaders, and staunch antagonists watched in disbelief as the impossible—a black man in the presidency—teetered on the cusp of reality.

I was pretty sure Obama would win. If I'd had any doubts, that four-hour early-voting line I stood in gave me a hint of victory. With a warm throng with water-cooler comedians for entertainment, the motley crew of African Americans lining the halls of Olive Harvey Community College spanned every walk of life. They waited patiently, albeit nervously, to cast their history-making vote. Passersby over the months had made a lot of biblical parallels with the election, comparing the forty years it took the Jews to get from the wilderness to the promised land to the forty years between Martin Luther King's death in 1968 and the pending 2008 Obama election. Even Obama himself joked at the Catholic Charities roast that he was not born in a manger as some said, but rather on Krypton. Even the more cynical voters felt there was something uniquely different about this election.

After the Jeremiah Wright fiasco, nasty Obama versus Clinton primaries, and the Palin obsession, people were sick of politics as usual. Top that off with a hellacious economic downturn, a housing-market crash, and mass layoffs, and change was more than a notion. It was a lifeline.

HATERISM MATTERS

"A black man will never become president" was reiterated as often as "knock, knock, guess who?" in the black community. It doubled as both a commentary on the nation's racist underpinnings and a troubling reminder that no matter the level of education and success a person of color could reach in the United States, race would always be his or her greatest hurdle.

But the statement was repeated so frequently—half jokingly, half cynically—that it spoke to a widespread unwillingness to believe otherwise. Despite the presidential bids of Jesse Jackson, Al Sharpton, and others, the possibility of victory seemed distant. Institutional racism would continue, blacks would always be among the have-nots, and the only way to amass political clout was to hobnob with, be knighted by, or be the pupil of heavyweights who would never let your ambitions supersede theirs.

The possibilities of what it means to have an African American president can be explored only if you accept that an African American can in fact become president. P. Diddy himself, an entertainment mogul and business whiz, admitted that as a kid he wanted to be president, but he never shared it with anyone because he knew people would laugh. America at large didn't think it was possible. While many people wanted Obama to win, the only person besides Obama himself who absolutely knew he would win seemed to be Oprah, who in a lightning-bolt epiphany boldly suggested he run long before Obama appeared on the national political radar.

This impossible dream in black circles spoke to a fear to believe, a fear of disappointment, and a fear of backlash all rooted in the woeful disappointments of the past: the assassinations of King, the Kennedys, and Medgar Evers; the lynchings of liberators; the blackballing of freedom fighters; the character assassinations of those who bucked the system. While these events were some forty years removed, the memories loomed like London fog. Couple them with an unjustified war, police harassment, driving while black, housing discrimination, job discrimination, the inability to get loans, and systemic crime in urban areas—all routine problems that weren't sexy enough for news coverage and typically got shoved under the mass-consciousness rug. If that undercurrent didn't boil the blood, the hellacious federal response to New Orleans, when the nation watched an American city and its poor black citizens drown for days, was a disturbing reminder that race still mattered.

Hundreds of thousands of voters punched "yes" for change, but what that change meant with regard to race was riddled with as much fear as it was hope.

For the record, some African Americans weren't ready for progressive change, in whatever form it took. And if they were, they certainly didn't want Obama to lead it.

I don't have a problem with people choosing to vote as they please. Voting is personal. Blacks are not obligated to vote for black candidates and aren't obligated to express an allegiance to him or her if the candidate is not qualified. The Clintons had initiated a number of progressive policies and cultivated a strong relationship with African Americans during their political tenure. John Edwards, too, was an upstanding candidate who fought for the working class. A vote for any of them was not a cataclysmic setback. But as the candidates announced their bids, a large number of blacks who favored Clinton or Edwards weren't pointing to the virtue of their policies over Obama's. Even clear-cut Clinton allegiance due to past commitments would have made sense as an argument. Congressman Charles Rangel of New York, for example, referred to Hillary Clinton as New York's favorite daughter. As part of the New York

Democratic Party circle, his support of her was logical, as was the support of other political heavyweights.

But these were not the arguments that black Clinton supporters used. The primary reason that was scuttle-bucketing itself on talk shows and in e-mail blasts and chat rooms could be whittled down to the "who the hell does this black man think he is" factor. Other arguments, like he's inexperienced or too young, were just bullet points for the former.

The first reason for annoyance with Obama's bid seemed to be his lightning-quick rise. The same self-proclaimed black gate-keepers who'd praised his senatorial bid were highly suspicious of his quest for the presidency. Call it crabs in a barrel, jealousy, or ill-placed rage, but some influential people of color were piping mad that Obama even thought he could be president, with their biggest beef being some invisible hoop of black political credibility he hadn't hopped through.

Is he black enough? became the black talk-circuit discussion of the month. A virtual bird with no wings, the argument fell flat because none of these critics could explain what being black meant. Nor did they see the irony in charging that a black person voting for a black man with a solid voting record for president made them sellouts.

The most famous black critic on record was Tavis Smiley. A longtime national talk-show host who has positioned himself as an advocate for issues facing the black community, Smiley was uncharacteristically critical of Obama. He blasted Obama for not appearing at Jena 6 protests, for not appearing at the Black State of the Union televised vehicle that Smiley created, and for a widespread failure to discuss "black issues" on the campaign trail.

What began as mild critical analysis soared to the level of haterism as it became evident that Smiley just flat out didn't like

Obama's audacity to hope that he could hold the highest office in the land. From an observer's view it seemed almost personal, as Smiley hammered Obama day after day in radio segments, chipping away not at his policies or politics but at Obama's blackness. E-mail chains forwarding Smiley's anti-Obama rhetoric became blogger fodder. Talk about being on the wrong side of history! But Smiley was just the most visible naysayer, a stance he paid for when radio listeners and TV viewers flooded him with letters denouncing his unfounded disdain.

But there were others. Some famous, some not. At a meeting of African American journalists and political strategists I attended at the onset of Obama's candidacy, each political strategist on the panel was frighteningly anti-Obama, a shock to the eager audience. But their anger wasn't related to his policies or platform but rather the fact that he even thought he was qualified. The criticisms were downright nasty. Here you have credible, accomplished political strategists resorting to race and colorism idioms to again question this issue of blackness.

"What kind of black man raises that kind of money?"

"I'd question any black man who whites are so willing to support."

"He has a little bit of white in him, and you know what that means."

What? It was the most disheartening panel I'd ever attended, and a resounding *What decade is this?* echoed in my head. But the strategists rambled on and on, tossing one backward, coded color comment after another while basking in the glow of Hillary Clinton's political halo. I couldn't figure out which angered them more—the fact that Obama was running or the fact that he hadn't chosen any of the panelists in question to be on his team. But in retrospect, who would choose this bunch of malignant critics to be part of his or her campaign of change?

In another instance I overheard a conversation among self-designated glitterati on the day Obama announced his presidential bid. The conversation was mostly anger-filled commentary stating that Obama better remember "he's ours," and I assume that he'd better not make another move without consulting them in his progress. Which made me wonder, *Why the heck would he have to consult them to do anything?*

But this group of anti-Obama African Americans was oddly vocal, hopping from one radio station to the next belittling his nerve to run. They were so vocal that the mainstream media came under the illusion that the black community had split down the middle before the primaries. But it hadn't. The split existed only among the ranks of visible pundits.

Obama's Iowa primary win squashed much of this chatter, with fence hoppers figuring that if all-white Iowa could vote for him, surely Chicago's South Side, Watts, and every other black urban and rural pocket could. But the mumbling continued, the mainstream media picked up on it, and the highly hyped question in the early days of the primaries was *Will blacks vote for Obama?* which led to disturbing nightly news discussions on Obama's black credibility. Can the average black person vote for a biracial Ivy Leaguer? Is Obama too professorial for the black working class? The analysis was absurd and again made the faulty assumption that black people were mostly working-class idiots who resented educated people at their own expense. All eyes turned to South Carolina to get the pulse of the black voter. Would they go with Clinton or Obama?

The argument was irritating to say the least. A girlfriend and I were drinking margaritas at a Mexican restaurant days before the South Carolina primary when a very sad Puerto Rican guy pulled up a seat beside us. He was devastated, he said, because he just didn't understand why black people wouldn't vote for Obama. "Where did you get that from?" I asked, knowing good and well his assumption came from the glut of cable news stories using hearsay and racial stereotypes to deconstruct the black vote. When we reassured him that Obama would win South Carolina hands down, he just shook his head in sorrow. "Why don't black people like Obama? He seems like such a nice man." He was nearly in tears. Our attempts to cheer him up were fruitless, and he wandered back to the bar for another round.

Obama did win South Carolina, and the *Is he black enough?* question was silenced and trumped with the even more controversial *Is he too black?* with critics pointing to his affiliation with Trinity Church of Christ and the now notorious Reverend Jeremiah Wright, whose black theology and the adoption of Christianity as a symbol of the disenfranchised toppling the establishment had become front-page news.

Wright has been analyzed enough; his "God damned America" quip was worse than Chinese drip torture the way it was hashed and rehashed. The video was omnipresent, replayed like a winning touchdown on cable news. Wright's defense at the Press Club was downright confusing as he played into the hands of Obama's competitors.

But the collective media-focus flip from *Is Obama black enough?* to *Is he too black?* in less than a week was one of the craziest turnabouts in political history. Obama had to refute and deny Wright. He had to refute and deny Louis Farrakhan, a latter-day rite of passage for every black politician on the national stage. Obama was linked to Bill Ayers, a 1960s radical who bombed federal buildings in political protest and later went on to become a respected professor. "I don't think I should be blamed for something a man did when I was eight years old," Obama said.

If baptism by fire via the Wright fiasco wasn't enough, the next attempt to play up Obama's blackness turned his knack for public speaking into a flaw. Since Obama's Democratic Convention speech in 2004, he's been heralded as a riveting speaker. His ability to inspire large crowds with rousing speeches speaking to the glories of democracy and aspiration frightened competitors. While this ability to touch the hearts of masses was dumbed down by critics as nothing more than mesmerism, his political aptitude was minimalized to mere speechmaking. Obama was not a skilled civic leader but rather an orator in the vein of Jackson, Sharpton, King, and Wright and in the league of black preachers and politicians at large. The word "orator" was increasingly used by TV pundits and became doublespeak for "black," as if to say, Well, they all give good speeches, but what do they do? He gives such nice speeches, pundits sneered. Oratorical skill, a talent widely respected in black communities, which have a penchant for preachers, politicians, and spirited teachers, was knocked.

But the biggest haterism moment came when Jesse Jackson, former presidential candidate, hero, and longtime mouthpiece for black America, was caught on mic on the news calling Obama the n-word and remarking that he wanted to, in so many words, castrate him for giving speeches on absent dads to black audiences. The action cost Jackson a speech at the Democratic convention, clouded his legacy, and, despite Obama's public forgiveness, forged a wedge between the two biggest black heroes in the political sphere. It trumped Clinton's racially tinged off-the-cuff reference to Robert Kennedy's assassination. Pick your poison—castration or assassination.

Atlanta congressman John Lewis, a staunch Clintonite, switched his vote to Obama. A civil rights leader who went on to politics, Lewis said he couldn't let this moment pass without doing "what was right." And he went on record to say so.

Today, few people in black circles would say that they did not vote for Obama or even questioned voting for him. Any criticism of Obama could get you stonewalled.

PALINISM

So Obama went from being unqualified to not black enough to too black and a terrorist sympathizer before snagging the Democratic nomination. The Republican Party's torpedoes upped the ante, making Obama not just a terrorist sympathizer but a terrorist himself. Obama was labeled "un-American" and "unpatriotic," and Republican-friendly Internet bloggers charged that Obama wasn't American at all. This was followed by charges that his policies were socialist, and two weeks before the election, in a throwback to U.S. history class, the term "communist" was hurled. Obama was a red-blooded communist? I can't remember the last time communism was used as some red-flag word, outside of scant references to China and Cuba, to rile the American public. Again, what decade did they think this was?

I don't know what their logic was in bringing Governor Sarah Palin on as the Republican vice-presidential nominee. It's incredibly multifaceted. Senator John McCain's maverick status received a booster shot when he was praised for taking the gamble of a lifetime with a fresh, conservative unknown from Alaska with some system-bucking of her own under her belt. Initially, Palin's selection bolstered hopes of securing those women who had supported

Clinton. Some speculated that she matched Obama's soul-stirring charisma, looks, and charm, while others pointed to her hockey-mom stats and blue-collar background as rousing the working-class Republican base.

If nothing else, her meteoric rise and fall in a hair-raising general election campaign was a puzzling distraction from real issues. I was a blogging zealot, fast-forwarding to keep up with the daily Palin foibles, the Katie Couric interview, *Saturday Night Live* satires, and Internet gossip with an eye-gluing attention usually reserved for reality TV or *Desperate Housewives*. At Halloween, adults donned Palin wigs and glasses. Signs at the Republican convention proclaimed her a HOT VP FROM A COOL STATE, but touting her as a feminist or advocate for women's rights in light of her antichoice and anti–equal pay for women stances was laughable. Her ignorance of international affairs and domestic issues snowballed into a serious problem for McCain, with more attention devoted to her media escapades than to McCain's message. As Obama's lead solidified in the days leading up to the general election, Palin was blamed for the loss.

TRANSITION DYNAMICS

As the possibility of an Obama presidency became real, some rushed to shape the dialogue on the election's meaning. The most obvious assumption, based on the "a black man can't become president" logic, is that if one does make it to that rank (presuming he won't be killed, the other half to the downer twist), then racism must be over. So out came a steady wave of speakers and pundits on black talk radio who wanted to reassure black America that if Obama did win, don't get too excited, because racism still exists.

Among the larger fears was the possibility of the dismantling of affirmative action. If Obama won, would the country abandon all affirmative action and diversity initiatives? Affirmative action had taken a steady beating for nearly a decade, with universities and companies slowly rolling back measures and charging that affirmative action was discriminatory to white men. The U.S. Supreme Court upheld affirmative action in the nation's universities.

But even beyond the need for affirmative action, I wondered if any of the fearmongers had entertained the idea of a day when the government actually lived up to the Declaration of Independence's right to the pursuit of happiness, that far-off day when everyone did have equal access, and if they entertained the possibility of a day when we wouldn't need it at all.

What if, through some magic-wand action, an Obama presidency ended institutional racism. Then what?

That notion seemed equally as troubling, and no one wanted to talk about it.

BLACK POWER IN A NEW AGE

Since the 1970s the issue of black empowerment has been rooted on the strength of longtime black institutions, businesses, churches, and agencies. Power was amassed through new political might in cities and governments, rising power brokers in corporate America. While the Black Power movement was never exclusionary or specifically antiwhite, it was oriented to counter racism. But as power structures merged and political and economic strength grew and splintered, interest grew in centralizing this wealth.

With President Obama's history in the making, I wonder how this concept will morph? The focus of Black Power reportedly shifted from civil rights to financial empowerment, but is there another tier? Or is the concept itself riddled in ideologies with shifting relevance? At the heart, that's what this post black concept explores. How much of our identity is a summation of countering racism, and how much of it is authentically us? Not that the two can't coincide. Cultural pride is a source of personal empowerment, a building block for pride, a blueprint for change. But in this time of shifting identities, personal responsibility takes an upswing that bodes both incredible promise and awesome fear. The question *Who are we?* could very well be replaced with *Who am I?* And where do personal pursuits of dreams and happiness fall in the pantheons of cultural responsibility and empowerment? Returning to DuBois's double identity, being black and American is one thing, but being black and an individual is something else. As these individual pursuits change the social fabric, the definition of being black or African American will evolve as well.

Being black is not static. Black unfolds as we unfold. The next tier of evolution is, arguably for the first time, solely and totally up to us. It's no longer funneled and distorted by debilitating institutional racism. That can be worked around. It's no longer couched solely by life experiences in the rigors of the Deep South or the 'hood, although they have an influence, too. It is as worldly and as isolated as we make it. As mass-produced or indie as we choose. As commodifed as we allow it to be. No, while we aren't at the helm of media everywhere, our voice, more than ever before, can be our voice. President Obama, who embraces most of the nontraditional African American factors referenced in this book, campaigned for change but also serves as a symbol of these new, integrated ideas and how they play themselves out on the world stage. Is he the new black? Much like saying the new black is blue—besides sounding trite and trendy—such a notion implies that blackness is a perception that can be commodified and altered at will. But there's nothing invested, at least for African Americans, for blackness to be a painted mirage, either. And President Obama, while symbolizing many things for many people, is a man elected by the people and who makes decisions that affect the world every day. But the question is: What does this mean? Does it mean I can do anything? Does it mean I can be anybody? Does it mean the sky is the limit? Does it mean I can make change? These are the values put before African American kids, and American kids in general. If you work hard and work smart, you can do anything in this country. But we feared to believe this, despite those stellar many who did. If I can make any conclusion about an Obama presidency, it's that that fear and its basis have been removed. And what does that mean? It means that when we say "you can do anything," it's not followed by a "but" clause. It means you can, in fact, reach your highest possibilities.

When I canvassed the Indianapolis projects, there were a few toddlers playing outside of a woman's home. We were passing out OBAMA FOR PRESIDENT stickers, and my mom mashed one on a little kid's plastic truck. The kid, no more than four, looked at the sticker and pedaled off as far as he could, which was no more than a door or two down, before his mom called him to turn around and ride back. What will his world be like? What opportunities will he see that will defy his situation or surroundings? All of this, we will come to see. And I welcome the revelations.

ACKNOWLEDGMENTS

I would like to thank everyone whose unique voice made this book possible. Special thanks to editors Susan Betz and Lisa Reardon, as well as the entire Chicago Review Press staff, for taking this project on and making this book a reality.

SOURCES

INTRODUCTION

African Americans' opposition to the Iraq War was highly documented. Blogger Jill Tubman refers to a Gallup poll in her blog, JackandJillPolitics.com, that stated that 85 percent of African Americans opposed the war. She also states that African Americans largely opposed the war before its inception. www.jackandjillpolitics .com/2007/05/african-americans-on-the-iraq-war-the-military-and-electoral-impact/.

Condoleezza Rice was one of the highest-ranking African Americans to hold federal office. She is recognized as an astute woman with many gifts; her conservative views and her position in George W. Bush's cabinet, however, put her at odds politically with most African Americans. Eugene Robinson writes on this subject in "What Rice Can't See" in the *Washington Post*, October 24, 2005. www.washingtonpost.com/wp-dyn/content/article/2005/10/24/ AR2005102401370.html.

On November 4, 2007, National Public Radio reported a Pew Research Center study showing that only 20 percent of African Americans thought they were better off than they were five years ago. www.npr.org/templates/story/story.php?storyId = 16284357.

Sam Roberts discusses the growing number of African immigrants in the *New York Times* article "More Africans Enter U.S. than in Days of Slavery." Roberts also details some of the challenges between African-born and native-born African Americans. www .nytimes.com/2005/02/21/nyregion/21africa.html?ex = 1109653200 &en = c164ab867f6bf987&ei = 5070.

I interviewed Mauricio Valesquez, CEO of Diversity Training, for
the article "The New Diversity: Corporate America Says Hello to the
Generation Gap, Intra-Ethnic Issues, Disabilities, and Religion in the
Workplace," in *NV* (New Vision in Business) magazine's December/
January 2008 issue, pp. 24–33. Valesquez said that intra-ethnic conflicts are a rising issue in the workplace. I also interviewed Harvard
University sociology professor Frank Dobbins. Dobbins authored a
study showing the ineffectiveness of day-long diversity seminars in
corporate America, arguing that such programs aren't enough.

A genealogy study revealed that activist Al Sharpton is the
descendent of slaves owned by the great-grandfather of former
segregationist senator Strom Thurmond. www.washingtonpost
.com/wp-dyn/content/article/2007/02/25/AR2007022501518
.html. News reports also showed that President Obama and former
vice president Dick Cheney are distant cousins. www.suntimes.com/
news/politics/obama/familytree/545460,BSX-News-wotreea09
.article.

In 2007 the Cherokee Nation voted to oust a coalition of blacks
and multiracials known as the Freedmen from their rosters. Jeninne
Lee-St. John covered the fallout in the *Time* article "The Cherokee
Nation's New Battle," which ran Thursday, June 21, 2007. www
.time.com/time/nation/article/0,8599,1635873,00.html.

The Jena 6 protests were covered extensively. Democracy Now!
was one of dozens of advocacy groups that provided information on
the case. www.democracynow.org/2007/7/10/the_case_of_the_jena_six.

*The Peebles Principles: Tales and Tactics from an Entrepreneur's
Life of Winning Deals, Succeeding in Business, and Creating a For-
tune from Scratch* by R. Donahue Peebles with J. P. Faber (Hoboken:
John Wiley and Sons, 2007). I had the pleasure of interviewing
Peebles for *NV* magazine, "The Peebles Principles," December/
January 2008, pp. 42–48.

The number of businesses owned by African American women skyrocketed over the past decade. Jim Hopkins writes about the change in *USA Today*, "African-American Women Step Up in Business World," August 24, 2006. www.usatoday.com/money/smallbusiness/2006-08-24-women-biz-usat_x.htm.

DeNeen L. Brown writes about Janks Morton's film *What Black Men Think* in the *Seattle Times* article "Filmmaker Tries to Debunk Labels of Black Men," August 15, 2007. http://seattletimes.nwsource.com/html/movies/2003836145_blackmen15.html.

The Associated Press released a Census Bureau report asserting that three times as many black people live in prisons than in college dorms, September 27, 2007. The AP story notes that commuter students were not included. www.msnbc.msn.com/id/21001543/. The *Baltimore Sun*'s Michael Strambler wrote an op-ed on the subject, titled "Are More Black Men Really in Jail than in College?" October 11, 2007.

The Economic Policy Institute challenges reports that the African American graduation rate is 50 percent, pointing to a number of variables that aren't included in the assessment. The National Education Longitudinal Study (NELS) estimates that the African American graduation rate is closer to 79 percent. www.epi.org/publications/entry/book_grad_rates/.

The *Navy Times* ran an AP story reporting that the Southern Regional Education Board found that the number of blacks enrolled in college has risen by more than half over the last decade and now makes up 21 percent of college students in the region. African Americans make up only 21 percent of the regional population. www.navytimes.com/careers/college/military_black_collegeenrollment_070628/.

The National Endowment for the Arts reports that reading rates for African Americans were up 15 percent since 2002. National

book reading rates are up for the nation. http://arts.endow.gov/
news/news09/ReadingonRise.html.

R. Drew Smith, author of *Long March Ahead: African American
Churches and Public Policy in Post–Civil Rights America*, volume 2
(Durham, NC: Duke University Press, 2005), discusses the church's
changing role. The shift away from activism was also noted in *Social
Witness, 'Prophetic' Discernment, and Post–Civil Rights Era Church-
es*, a report by Smith on a roundtable discussion among African
American ministers at the Leadership Center at Morehouse College
in Spring 2001. www.rcno.org/SocialWitness_DrewSmith.pdf.

A federal jury found that New York Knicks coach Isiah Thomas
sexually harassed Anucha Brown Sanders, a former team executive. In a deposition, Thomas said that a white man calling a black
woman a bitch was worse than a black man doing the same thing.
National Public Radio reported the story on October 3, 2007. www
.npr.org/templates/story/story.php?storyId = 14945034.   Thomas
was later fired. On April 12, 2007, CBS Radio fired white radio
shock jock Don Imus for calling the mostly black Rutgers wom-
en's basketball team "nappy-headed 'hos." www.cbsnews.com/
stories/2007/04/12/national/main2675273.shtml.

On July 9, 2007, the NAACP held a mock funeral for the *n*-word.
The service took place at the 98th Annual Convention in Detroit,
Michigan. www.naacp.org/events/convention/98th/funeral/index
.htm. Months later, rapper Nas announced that his latest CD would
be titled *Nigger*. The announcement was made on October 17, 2007,
to great controversy. The album was released in summer 2008 as
an untitled LP. Allhiphop.com discussed the controversy and Nas's
unlikely supporters including Don Imus. http://allhiphop.com/
stories/news/archive/2007/10/17/18746861.aspx.

1 THE GENERATION GAP: THE YOUNG BLACK PROFESSIONAL

A research paper authored by Howard University graduate students explores generational divides. "Teaching the Millennials: An Exploration of Curriculum, Diversity, Technology, and Natural Disasters" by Nere Ayu, Angela Henderson, Karen Miller, Valerie Stackman, and Veronica Womack, December 2008.

2 THE AFRICAN DIASPORA: NEW IMMIGRANTS IN AFRICAN AMERICA

Rachel L. Swarns highlights the unique relationship between U.S.-born and African-born blacks in the *New York Times* story "'African American' Becomes a Term for Debate," which ran August 29, 2004. www.nytimes.com/2004/08/29/us/african-american-becomes-a-term-for-debate.html?pagewanted = all.

I interviewed young college women on their thoughts about music and sexuality for "The Beat Goes On: Female Hip-Hop Fans Look Past Misogyny." The article appeared in the May 26, 2004, edition of the *Chicago Tribune*. Their comments on Africa were not included.

African immigrant education levels were reported in the article "African Immigrants in the United States Are the Nation's Most Highly Educated Group," *Journal of Blacks in Higher Education*, no. 26 (Winter 1999, 2000) pp. 60–61.

Sam Green covered African migration in the story "More African Immigrants Enter U.S. than in Days of Slavery," *New York Times*, February 21, 2005. www.nytimes.com/2005/02/21/nyregion/21africa.html.

The United African Organization provides resources for African immigrants in the metropolitan Chicago area. http://uniteafricans .org/site/index.php.

"The Politics of Braids" by Tasneem Paghdiwala deconstructs the African braiders vs. African American hair care industry debate. The story ran in the *Chicago Reader* on September 1, 2007. www.chicagoreader.com/chicago/the-politics-of-braids/Content?oid = 923019.

3 BRIDGES: BIRACIAL, BICULTURAL IDENTITY

I wrote "I'm Not White" for *Ebony* magazine's August 2007 issue. The story features the life experiences of light-skinned African Americans who were frequently mistaken for being white.

4 BLACK, GAY, LESBIAN, AND PROUD: GLBT IN BLACK AMERICA

I wrote the story "Down Low Revelations Stir Fear; Caution," which ran in the *Chicago Tribune*, June 30, 2004. The story followed J. L. King, author of the controversial book *On the Down Low: A Journey into the Lives of "Straight" Black Men Who Sleep with Men* (New York: Broadway Books, 2004), as he talked to a crowd of largely African American women about DL lifestyles.

Widespread reports stated that 70 percent of African Americans voted in support of Proposition 8, a ban on same-sex marriage in the state of California. Voters made the decision on the same day they elected President Barack Obama. The *Los Angeles Times* November 8 story "70 percent of African Americans Backed Prop 8, Exit Poll Finds" refers to an Associated Press exit poll. http://latimesblogs .latimes.com/lanow/2008/11/70-of-african-a.html. However, another study states that those statistics are grossly exaggerated. In the January 9, 2009, edition of Salon.com, Alex Koppelman refers to a study by Patrick J. Egan of New York University and Kenneth Sherrill of Hunter College. In a precinct-level statistical analysis of the vote, Egan and Sherrill found the vote to be 58 percent in support of Proposition 8. www.salon.com/politics/war_room/2009/01/09/race_prop8/.

7 BLACK ENTREPRENEURS: NEW URBAN IMPRESARIOS AND POSTRACIAL SHOPKEEPERS

"Magic vs. Michael: Who Is the Better Entrepreneur" was written by Megan Scott for *NV* magazine's June/July 2007 issue. The article credits both athletes with changing the dynamics of entrepreneurship.

I interviewed Ernel Dawkins for *NV* magazine. The story, titled "Kickin' It," ran in the October 2008 issue.

I interviewed Celeste Johnny for the story "Swim Season" in the April/May 2009 issue of *NV* magazine.

Orneno Wright's story on Dr. Susan Taylor of RX for Brown Skin, titled "Celebrating Hue: Filling a Skin Care Niche," ran in *NV* magazine's April/May 2009 issue.

I interviewed several business owners and professionals in "The Conversation: Black Owned vs. Majority Owned and Urban Marketed" for *NV* magazine's February 2006 issue. Participants discussed their dual responsibilities as black consumers.

Megan Scott wrote "The Remix: Black-Owned Mom and Pop Shops Are Struggling to Maintain Customers While Large Chains Infiltrate Urban America" for *NV* magazine's Februrary 2006 issue. Scott highlights the new challenges that black-owned small businesses face.

8 TALENTED TENTH REVISITED: CAPITALISM VERSUS SOCIAL RESPONSIBILITY

I wrote a story on Generation X perspectives on the talented tenth, titled "The Talented Tenth: Social Responsibility vs. Elitism," which appeared in the February/March 2007 issue of *NV* magazine, pp. 28–33. Several interviews from this story appeared in the chapter.

W. E. B. DuBois's classic *The Souls of Black Folk*, written in 1903 (Chicago: A. C. McClurg & Co.), introduced the highly debated talented tenth concept.

9 NEOFEMINISM: WOMANIST VALUES IN THE AGE OF THE VIDEO GIRL

Quarterlife Crisis: The Unique Challenges of Life in Your Twenties by Alexandra Robbins and Abby Wilner (New York: Penguin Putnam, 2001) compared the stress of early adulthood and new millennium pressures to the suffering of those in midlife crisis. I wrote about this issue and how it affects young black women in the article "Great Expectations," *Honey* magazine, November 2001.

10 THE OBAMA FACTOR: REDEFINING POSSIBILITY

Michael Eric Dyson refers to cultural amnesia in the foreword to *Beats Rhymes and Life: What We Love and Hate About Hip Hop*, which I edited with Kenji Jasper (New York: Harlem Moon, 2007).

Mary Mitchell, columnist for the *Chicago Sun-Times*, wrote "Why Is Tavis Smiley Dissing Obama?" in the February 14, 2008, edition. Smiley's criticism made headlines nationwide. http://

blogs.suntimes.com/mitchell/2008/02/why_is_tavis_smiley_ dissing_se.html.

"Is Obama Black Enough?" written by Ta-Nehisi Paul Coates, appeared in *Time* magazine, Thursday, February 1, 2008. http:// www.time.com/time/nation/article/0,8599,1584736,00.html. The article pointed to several African American critics who claimed Obama was not truly black. Michelle Obama said the discussion on her husband's blackness was "silly" in a CNN News report that ran February 1, 2008. www.cnn.com/2008/POLITICS/02/01/michelle. obama/.

Congressman John Lewis, a longtime Hillary Clinton supporter and civil rights leader, switched his primary vote to Barack Obama, fanning growing support for Obama. The announcement was widely reported and also mentioned by Jamie Dupree, who covered the announcement for WSB radio on February 28, 2008. http:// wsbradio.com/blogs/jamie_dupree/2008/02/the-john-lewisbarack-obama-sag.html.

INDEX

Italicized page references indicate illustrations.

ABOUT THE AUTHOR

Ytasha L. Womack is a journalist, a filmmaker, and the coeditor
of the groundbreaking anthology
*Beats, Rhymes, and Life: What
We Love and Hate about Hip-Hop.*
Her directorial debut, *The Engage-
ment: My Phamily BBQ 2* (2006),
was nominated for Best Film at
the American Black Film Festival,
won rave reviews at the International Black Harvest Festival of
Film and Video, and was featured
in *Variety*, the *Chicago Sun-Times*, and the *Chicago Tribune*. Her film
Love Shorts (2005) won Best Film at the Truth Magazine Hip Hop
Awards, and she coproduced and wrote the Billboard-chart-topping
documentary *Tupac: Before I Wake* (SepiaTone Entertainment). A
current guest editor with *NV Magazine* and frequent contributor to
Ebony, she is a former editor at large with *Upscale* and former staff
writer for the *Chicago Defender*. Her work has appeared in *VIBE*,
Essence, Honey, Emerge, XXL, King, and the *Chicago Tribune* as well
as the comic book *Delete*. She has served as a commentator for
NBC-5 Chicago, CBS News, *Absolut Soulful Sundays*, and WVON
Radio. A graduate of Clark Atlanta University—a historically black
university—she lives in Chicago.

Conversate Is Not a Word
Getting Away from Ghetto
Jam Donaldson

978-1-55652-780-7
$14.95 ($16.95 CAN)

Funny, sad, angry, and refreshingly honest, this provocative commentary explores black culture and what needs to be done to fix neighborhoods and improve lives. Jam Donaldson is a provocateur of the most entertaining kind. She offers real actions people can take to improve their lives and black society overall, never taking a condescending, holier-than-thou tone. She weaves her own warring viewpoints—the internal struggle between Jam "the Negro" and Jam "the American"—a duality first spoken of by W. E. B. DuBois—into the discussion of what's wrong and what needs to be done to fix it. *Conversate Is Not a Word* is a call to action and a practical guide for responsible, personal activism.

Not All Black Girls Know How to Eat
A Story of Bulimia
Stephanie Covington Armstrong

978-1-55652-786-9
$16.95 ($18.95 CAN)

"Armstrong's intimate account of her battles with eating disorders shatters many longstanding myths and opens a space for those who have been silent for so long to speak . . . and be heard."
—Jaime Pressly, actress, *My Name Is Earl*, and author of *It's Not Necessarily Not the Truth*

In this insightful and moving first-person narrative, Armstrong describes her struggle as a black woman with a disorder that is consistently portrayed as a white woman's problem.